Echoes of History
The Patterns We Refuse to See

Most people believe they would recognize major societal change while it was happening.

History suggests otherwise.

Jerry M. Elman

ISBN: 979-8-9956196-0-4 (paperback)

ISBN: 979-8-9956196-1-1 (hardcover)

First edition

Printed in the United States of America

For my parents,

who survived what history became.

And for my children and granddaughter,

who deserve a world that still remembers how easily people can change without realizing it.

ACKNOWLEDGMENTS

No book is written alone, even when the work itself feels like it stems from a place no one else can enter.

I am grateful to the people who encouraged me to keep writing when the weight of history felt too heavy to carry forward—and to those who understood that this book is not a project, but a responsibility. Some offered feedback. Some offered time.

To my wife, family, and closest friends: thank you for giving me the space to dig into the past and the patience to put up with how it still burdens me. You have lived with my struggles, my silences, and the long shadow of this journey.

To my children and grandchildren: you will inherit truth—and the strength that comes with it.

To the readers of *Miracles Through Hell* who told me their own family stories, who shared their inherited questions, and who reminded me that trauma does not end with one generation—thank you. Your voices made it impossible to stop at one book.

To the survivors who never found the words, and to the second generation who grew up inside the echoes—I owe you the promise that the lessons will not disappear with us.

And finally, to those who believe books cannot change anything: history was shaped by people who believed the same thing.

CONTENTS

AUTHOR'S OPENING NOTE

This is not a political book.

I am a second-generation Holocaust survivor. I grew up in a house where silence said more than words ever could.

Where I learned early that people break long before nations do.

My parents did not talk about what they lived through.

But the damage lived on in them.

And in me.

That changes how you see the world.

When I hear anger rising between friends, watch families split over politics, or see neighbors begin to treat each other as enemies, I do not just hear arguments.

I hear echoes.

Not of ghettos and camps.

But of what came before them.

The part most people forget.

Because tyranny rarely begins with violence.

It begins with division.

Inside homes.

Inside communities.

I have seen that division in my lifetime more than once.

People who once sat together at holidays now refuse to speak.

I write this as the child of trauma—and the inheritor of a warning.

A warning that patterns matter more than headlines.

The most powerful societal changes rarely happen all at once.

They happen gradually—until people often fail to recognize how much they themselves are changing along with the world around them.

The language is familiar.

The fear is familiar.

And the thing we forget, every time?

We are not as different as those who profit from division want us to believe.

We are still the same human beings we have always been.

We all want to feel safe.

We all need to belong.

We all carry burdens we did not choose.

But the patterns are leading somewhere else.

Toward a world where everyone becomes the enemy.

Where truth becomes whatever our side claims it is.

Where disagreement begins to feel dangerous—and people start believing the country itself is broken.

That is how it begins.

Not with dictators.

But with the slow erosion of trust, empathy, and truth.

This book is not here to tell you what to think.

It is here to help you see what is already happening—and what history has warned us about before.

The choice is still ours:

Remember the lessons.

Or repeat the pattern.

When people stop seeing each other as human, the pattern returns.

PRELUDE: BEFORE YOU READ

It warns about what happens when sides become more important than society.

This book is about patterns—the kind that appear long before people realize anything is changing.

Today, we argue more about facts than ever before.

Facts are snapshots.

Patterns tell a story.

History mostly looks backward.

It tells us what happened.

It shows us where things may be heading—often long before people recognize the direction.

People before us lived through the moment when ordinary life changed —quietly, gradually—until the unthinkable became normal.

And the thing that frightens me most today?

Those patterns are back.

Not the same uniforms.

Not the same slogans.

But the same sequence:

Division.

Silence.

Normalization.

This is not theory.

It is a progression.

A gradual human process through which fear, exhaustion, silence, adaptation, and normalization quietly reshape how people think, act, relate to one another, and understand the world around them.

Most people do not recognize the full extent of those changes while living through them.

That is why the pattern repeats.

It doesn't begin with systems.

It begins with people—how we respond, what we tolerate, and what we choose not to confront.

"It can't happen here."

It always can.

Before you read further, ask yourself a few simple questions.

When you think about the tone of public life today, do you feel proud of the direction our norms have taken? Or do you sometimes wish we had held on to more of the ones that once guided us?

When someone disagrees with you, do you see another citizen with different ideas—or an opponent?

This book offers a mirror.

A mirror reflecting what happens when societies ignore the patterns already unfolding around them.

If the book has one message, it is this:

Follow the patterns.

They never lie.

FOLLOW THE PATTERNS

Every generation believes it sees the world clearly—
until it looks back
and wonders how it missed what was right in front of it.

Think about your own life for a moment.

The world you grew up in had its own rules,
its own truths,
its own sense of what was normal.

Families could disagree without becoming enemies.
Facts were things we could still point to.
Right and wrong felt different in our bones.

That world did not feel temporary.
It felt stable—like something that would continue without effort
because it always had.

Most of us did not question it.

We lived inside it the way people live inside weather—without noticing it until it changes.

Now ask yourself:

When did that change?

When did we stop believing that truth was something shared instead of something shaped by our whims?

We define truth differently now.
We define "normal" differently.
We define each other differently.

That shift did not arrive all at once.
It did not come with a single event or a single decision.
It accumulated—quietly—through habits, reactions, and small adjustments in how we responded to one another.

This book is different from most books.

It is about patterns—
how they form,
what they reveal,
and where they lead.

Events are real.
They happened.
They can be verified.

But what matters most
is not the event by itself.
It is the pattern it belongs to.

Patterns hold meaning.
They show direction.
They show accumulation.

They show consequence before consequence becomes obvious.

When patterns repeat long enough,
they become history.

And history teaches something simple:

The same patterns
lead to the same consequences.

In illness.
In finance.
In sports.
In life.
And in the life of a nation.

We look for patterns almost everywhere.

In weather.
In business.
In medicine.
In markets.
In games.

We study them.
We trust them.
We act on them.

But there is one place we resist seeing them:

In ourselves.

That is how history repeats.

We miss the one set of patterns that matters most—
the patterns that reshape our character,
our values,

our empathy,
and our courage.

And by the time we notice what changed,
we are already different people
living under different norms,
telling ourselves it all happened on its own.

But it didn't.

It happened one small compromise at a time.
One exception at a time.
One silence at a time.

Until the accumulation of those choices became a new normal—
and the old one no longer felt reachable.

When people stop seeing the patterns,
they start looking for explanations.

They blame other people.
They grow angry.
They create enemies to explain their unease.

That reaction feels natural.
It feels justified.

But it is often a sign that something deeper has already shifted—
something harder to see and harder to admit.

And slowly,
what was once a community
becomes frightened tribes.

But the explanation was always in the pattern.

Patterns don't lie.
They repeat.

They show us what we would rather not see:
How people before us made the same choices,
ignored the same warnings,
and convinced themselves
their time was different.

Follow the patterns.

The score only tells you what happened after the fact.
The pattern tells you what was happening all along.

In baseball, the truth is rarely in the final score alone.

It is in the swings.
The timing.
The mistakes.
The habits.
The small adjustments that reveal
where the game is really going.

The most serious fans study those patterns relentlessly—
because patterns tell the truth
before the scoreboard does.

Nations are no different.

The signs are always there.

The problem is not the absence of warning.
The problem is that most people only look at the score
after the game is already lost.

And one of today's new norms is this:

When the outcome is not what people wanted,
they do not just object.

They rage.
They threaten.
They treat reality itself as the enemy.

That reaction is not just political.
It is behavioral.

And behaviors—when repeated—become patterns.

Countries are not living beings.
They are reflections
of the people who shape them.

A country becomes what its people permit,
reward,
excuse,
and ignore.

It does not control us
unless we surrender that control.

We either guide its direction,
or we hand that role to others—
usually while telling ourselves someone else will handle it.

We trade vigilance for convenience.
We take freedom for granted.

And the people who crave control
always notice that opening.

The Constitution begins with three words:

We the People.

Not some of the people.
Not only the people we like.

A democracy survives
only when people still believe
they belong to the same "we."

But look at where we are now.

We divide the country into "us" and "them"
as if democracy can survive
without a shared "us."

That was when I began asking myself a question
I think every person in this country needs to ask:

What changed my old norms?

The ones that once guided how I treated other people,
how I listened,
how I respected differences,
how I recognized truth when I saw it.

Hate is now expressed and reinforced every day—
in institutions,
in media,
in social feeds,
in broken friendships,
and inside families that no longer know how to speak to each other.

None of this feels normal
when measured against the lives most of us have actually lived.

Do we ever stop to ask
whether the way we think, react, and behave
is being shaped by forces outside us

rather than by the values we once believed were our own?

There was a time
when I got caught in these new norms too.

In the anger.
In the judgment.
In the easy habit of demonizing people.

I forgot something basic.

That freedom of speech means people have the right
to say what I dislike.

That people have the right
to vote for whom they choose.

That disagreement is supposed to be protected—
not punished.

That even fears I disagreed with
still felt real to the people who held them.

And when I finally realized I had become part of the problem,
I saw the line I had crossed.

I was living inside the same patterns
I was trying to expose.

That realization frightened me.

Because I was no longer living by my own standards.

I was living by standards someone else had normalized for me—
and I had convinced myself they were mine.

What concerned me was not only what people believed.

It was how they were behaving.

They had not always been this way.
Neither had I.

We had once been part of the same "we."

And now we were acting like enemies.

That was when I learned something
that changed how I see everything:

If we stop focusing first on the people
and start focusing on the norms—
the patterns of behavior that shape all of us—
we can begin to find common ground again.

We can disagree without hate.
We can differ without division.

Because no one becomes unrecognizable overnight.

Patterns make them so.

That is how it happens.

Not because people wake up evil.
But because they slowly forget who they are
while fighting what they hate.

The pattern comes first.
The consequences follow.

2

WHEN SILENCE ALMOST WON

You don't need history to recognize this. You've felt it.

History rarely records the moments
when a nation catches itself in time.

And when it does,
it is often because one person
refuses to let silence finish the job.

Most of the time, those moments pass unnoticed—
because from the inside, they do not feel like turning points.

They feel like ordinary days under growing pressure.

On March 9, 1954,
the United States came closer than most people realize
to becoming a different country.

That night,
Edward R. Murrow

sat under the harsh lights of a television studio,
his hands visibly shaking as he prepared to speak.

Not as a politician.
Not as an activist.
But as a journalist
who understood that a pattern had already formed—
and was hardening.

Fear had already become ordinary.

People lost jobs quietly.
Friends stopped calling.
Careers ended without explanation.

Silence passed for wisdom.

One accusation—Communist—was enough
to erase a life.

Evidence did not matter.
Context did not matter.
Defense did not matter.
The accusation itself
carried punishment.

This did not happen all at once.

It spread gradually—through caution, through avoidance, through the
quiet decisions people made to protect themselves.

At the center of it all stood
Joseph McCarthy,
a man who understood something
history teaches again and again:

Fear does not need facts.
It only needs permission.

And almost every institution complied.

The press hesitated.
Universities purged.
Hollywood blacklisted.
Congress avoided confrontation.

Even
Dwight D. Eisenhower
chose caution over challenge.

This was not unique to one era.

It was a familiar human response.

Fear rarely presents itself as fear.

It calls itself security.
Patriotism.
Protection.

And people accept it
because resistance feels reckless
while silence feels responsible.

Murrow understood the danger of waiting.

He had seen it before.

Democracies do not implode all at once.

They erode quietly—
while people convince themselves
that what they are seeing is temporary.

Murrow and
Fred Friendly
did not rant.

They documented.

They used McCarthy's own words.

And they trusted the audience
to see what fear had taught them to ignore.

When the broadcast aired,
Murrow spoke calmly.

Without theatrics.
Without outrage.

He reminded Americans:

Dissent is not disloyalty.
Accusation is not evidence.
Fear is not leadership.

When it ended,
the phones rang.

Not with anger.
With recognition.

People already knew something was wrong.
They just needed someone
to say it out loud.

McCarthy did not fall that night.

But something broke.

And once a pattern cracks,
it becomes harder to sustain.

Murrow did not stop history.

He interrupted it.

And that was enough.

3

AMERICA HAS ALWAYS TAKEN

For a long time, I thought what we were living through was unprecedented.

The openness of the cruelty.
The confrontations in the streets.
Force displayed instead of hidden.
The absence of embarrassment.

It felt like something had broken.

Eventually, I had to admit something harder:

It only feels shocking
if you grew up believing
that a brief period of restraint and expanding rights
represented a permanent transformation of America.

I did.
Many of us did.

We came of age during a relatively short period in American history

when empathy expanded,
when restraint mattered,
and when progress felt real.

Civil rights.
Women's rights.
Broader opportunity.

A growing sense that the country—while imperfect—
was moving in the right direction.

That period shaped how we understood America.
It shaped what we expected from it.
And it shaped what we believed was normal.

But it did not define America.

America has always been an experiment—
not only in democracy,
but in how much can be taken
while still claiming moral ideals.

That experiment has never moved in a straight line.

It moves in cycles.

Cruelty does not disappear here.
It pauses.
It reshapes itself.
Then it returns.

Once I began looking at the present through that lens,
it stopped feeling chaotic
and started feeling familiar.

America has always taken.

From the beginning, taking came first.

Land was taken.
Labor was taken.
Resources were taken.
Power was taken.

And just as important as any of that,
the story was taken too—
the story of who America is
and what it stands for.

This is not a moral accusation.
It is a historical pattern.

And like all patterns, it is visible only when you step back far enough to
see repetition instead of isolated events.

Indigenous land was taken, not negotiated.

Enslaved labor was not a side effect of prosperity.
It was central to it.

Immigrant labor was welcomed
when it could be used cheaply,
controlled easily,
and discarded when no longer needed.

What changed over time
was not the behavior.
It was the explanation.

America does not move forward in a straight line.

It expands.
Takes.

Stabilizes briefly.
Then tightens again.

First, it takes to fuel growth.
Then, it justifies the taking
with ideals—freedom, opportunity, destiny.

Those ideals matter.
They are not meaningless.

But they are often applied unevenly—expanded in some moments,
restricted in others.

When pressure builds and instability follows,
the system loosens just enough to survive.

Empathy expands briefly,
not always because it is cherished,
but because it becomes necessary.

And when expectations grow too large,
the system corrects itself.

Harder.
Colder.
More openly.

Cruelty does not vanish.
It waits.

Early on, America learned how to separate ideals from behavior.

Liberty was declared while slavery expanded.
Equality was promised while exclusion was enforced.
Opportunity was advertised while access was controlled.

The ideals became something to believe in.
Reality became something to live with.

That separation allowed people to function inside contradiction.

The story softened the taking.
The poetry made the harm easier to tolerate.

It worked.

One of the strongest myths America ever created
was that immigrants were welcomed here.

They were not.

The Irish were despised.
Italians were criminalized.
Jews were blocked by quotas.
Chinese immigrants were legally excluded.

Mexican laborers were brought in when needed
and pushed out when convenient.

What changed was not the treatment.
The story changed.

Emma Lazarus's poem "The New Colossus," engraved on the Statue of
Liberty,
did not describe America as it was.

It described America
as it wanted to imagine itself.

People embraced that image
because it made participation feel moral—
even when reality lagged far behind it.

The poem stood.
The detentions continued.
The exclusions continued.
The inspections continued.

America learned early
that it could take in practice
while telling a different story—
and most people would accept the story
because they needed to.

Cruelty in America has rarely been loud.

Most of the time, it has been administrative.
Lawful.
Routine.
Structured.

Whether enforced through slave patrols,
removal orders,
exclusion laws,
labor crackdowns,
or modern methods of enforcement,
the function has remained the same:

Decide who belongs.
Take what is needed.
Discard the rest.

This kind of cruelty does not always require hatred.
It requires efficiency.

Another moment in history made this impossible to ignore.

During World War II,
Japanese American citizens—many of them born in this country—

were rounded up and placed in camps.

Families had their homes taken.
Their businesses taken.
Their freedom taken.

There was no individualized guilt.
No due process.

Only categorization and fear.

It was done legally.
And with broad public acceptance.

This was not mob violence.

It was orderly.
Bureaucratic.
Efficient.

And it happened in a period
we still prefer to remember as a moral high point.

That contradiction matters.

It shows that even when a nation believes it is acting justly,
the underlying pattern can still operate—quietly, structurally, and with
public consent.

Politicians did not invent this system.
They learned how to survive inside it.

Over time, political survival required something more refined:
Managing public discomfort.

They learned how to speak about compassion

while enforcing hardness.

How to praise ideals
while protecting structures built on taking.

How to express concern
without accepting responsibility.

The outcomes remained.
The language changed.

Every major expansion of rights in America
followed the same pattern.

Civil rights.
Women's rights.
Disability rights.
LGBTQ rights.

None were granted easily.
All were resisted.

And all were treated as dangerous
once they began to work.

These movements did more than expand access.

They changed expectations.
They changed who could reasonably expect dignity.

And that shift created tension.

For a time, empathy expanded.

Laws changed.
Access widened.
Visibility grew.

But empathy creates expectations.

And expectations threaten structures built on taking.

So the system tolerated progress—
until it didn't.

After World War II, something unusual happened.

For a brief period, American ideals and American behavior
came closer than they ever had.

Education expanded.
Homeownership expanded.
Labor protections strengthened.
Public investment benefited the many.

This was not pure moral awakening.
It was also practical.

The world had just seen where industrialized cruelty leads.

Shared sacrifice created shared obligation.

For a while, empathy was not optional.
It made sense.

And that period became the America
many people still think of as normal.

It wasn't.

As dignity expanded, expectations expanded.

And eventually, resistance followed.

Slowly, the language changed.

Public good became waste.

Solidarity became dependency.
Restraint became weakness.

The shift did not happen in one election,
one policy,
or one movement.

It happened across time—through accumulated reactions to change.

The election of
Barack Obama
was celebrated as a milestone—and it was.

But structurally, it crossed a line
it had never been fully comfortable with.

For many people,
this did not feel symbolic.

It felt like loss.

Loss of certainty.
Loss of ownership.
Loss of control over who America was for.

What followed was not accidental.

First came obstruction.
Then normalization.
Then correction.

Empathy was reframed as excess.
Inclusion as threat.
Rights as overreach.

This was not just about policy.

It was about boundaries.
Control.
And identity.

That is why today feels so extreme.

Not because it is new.

Because it violates expectations
shaped by a rare period of restraint.

If we compare the present
to earlier periods in American history—open exclusion, unapologetic
force, systemic removal—
the shock begins to fade.

What feels like an ending
is, in many ways, a return.

What is new is the openness.
The confrontation.
The absence of shame.

Force is no longer hidden behind paperwork.
It is visible.
Televised.
Normalized.

Cruelty has become a signal of seriousness.
Empathy is treated as disorder.

That shift does not require a new ideology.
It requires incentives.

American prosperity has always depended on taking—
including taking control of meaning.

Who belongs.
Who is blamed.
Who is deserving.
Who benefits.

The ideals were never entirely false.
But they were never fully paid for either.

Believing in the ideals softens the taking.
It does not stop it.

America has never lacked ideals.

It has struggled to live by them.

That is the pattern.

And the danger comes
when cruelty is treated
as proof that the system is working.

That line has been crossed before.

History keeps asking the same question—
in different words,
in different uniforms,
in different moments:

Do we recognize the pattern—
or do we take again?

But before patterns shape nations, they shape something smaller. They
shape people.

4

SEEING IS NO LONGER BELIEVING

Authoritarian regimes evolve.

When intimidation stops working,
they do not retreat.

They change the terrain.

The next terrain is reality itself.

This shift does not happen suddenly.

It develops over time, as people become accustomed to questioning not just interpretation, but the existence of truth itself.

For most of modern history,
disagreement followed a recognizable structure.

People argued about interpretation.
About meaning.
About intent.

But they largely agreed
on what had happened.

That agreement no longer holds.

We used to share something simple:

A basic understanding of what was real.

Not agreement—
reality.

Facts were things you could verify.
Things that happened
whether you liked them or not.

Opinions were how we interpreted those facts.

Beliefs came from somewhere deeper—
identity,
experience,
values we often did not examine.

Those three things once lived in tension.

Now they are collapsing into each other.

Opinions are treated like facts.
Beliefs are defended like evidence.
Facts are dismissed
when they threaten identity.

That shift is not just intellectual.
It is behavioral.

It changes how people respond, how they listen, and whether they are
willing to accept information that contradicts what they already
believe.

And once that shift takes hold,
disagreement no longer functions the same way.

That is not disagreement.

That is the breakdown of reality itself.

We are living in a moment
when people can watch events unfold—
recorded in real time,
from multiple angles,
by countless witnesses—
and still be persuaded
that what they saw
was not real,
not representative,
or not happening at all.

Access to information is not the problem.

It is happening at a time
when more information is available
than at any point in human history.

And yet, confidence in what is true
has weakened.

January 6 is the clearest example
because the event was so visible.

Millions watched the footage.

Crowds breaching barricades.
Police officers beaten.
Lawmakers fleeing.
Windows shattered.
Threats shouted.

Gallows erected.

Much of it was recorded
by the participants themselves.

And yet almost immediately,
a counter-story emerged—
not merely arguing over meaning,
but questioning whether the event was violent,
coercive,
or even an attack at all.

People were told:

The footage was misleading.
The scenes were exaggerated.
The participants were peaceful.
The violence was staged.
The video lacked context.

That response matters.

Because it signals a shift away from debating interpretation
toward questioning whether shared evidence has any authority at all.

That shift matters.

Because once a population can be trained
to distrust direct visual evidence,
power no longer needs to hide.

It only needs repetition.

This chapter is not about proving intent
or assigning partisan blame.

It is about recognizing a behavioral pattern
that appears across eras and ideologies—
and understanding what that pattern makes possible.

When reality itself becomes unstable,
accountability becomes harder to enforce.

And when accountability weakens,
power expands with less resistance.

The pattern does not end with denial.

It becomes more efficient.

"The protesters are paid."

That sentence has become
one of the most effective tools
for dissolving reality
without ever having to refute it.

It does not address the facts.

It removes the need to.

If protesters are "paid,"
then dissent is artificial.
Outrage is manufactured.
Suffering is staged.
Resistance is not real.

Once that frame is accepted,
no further moral reckoning is required.

The video no longer has to be evaluated.
The grievance no longer has to be heard.
The abuse no longer has to be confronted.

The people on screen
are no longer citizens.

They are props.

This shift simplifies decision-making.

It allows people to disengage
without feeling responsible for what they are seeing.

This maneuver appears again and again—
in labor protests,
racial justice demonstrations,
immigration protests,
student movements,
climate activism.

The context changes.
The mechanism does not.

Attention shifts
from what is happening
to who is funding it.

From substance
to suspicion.

From moral reckoning
to withdrawal.

That shift is subtle,
but its effect is significant.

It replaces engagement with distance.

That phrase has power
because it relieves responsibility.

Once people believe what they are seeing is staged,
they no longer ask
why others are risking arrest, livelihood, or safety.

They no longer ask
what conditions produced such anger.

They step back.
Comfortably.

The same pattern now appears
in responses to videos
showing harsh or abusive conduct
by immigration enforcement.

Footage that in another era
might have triggered immediate moral reckoning
is instead minimized, reframed, or dismissed.

The details vary.

The pattern does not:

The footage is isolated.
The footage lacks context.
The victims are not credible.
The conduct is necessary.
The video cannot be trusted.

Reality is not disproved.

It is diluted.

History offers precedent.

Authoritarian systems rarely rely on lies alone.

They rely on confusion.

The goal is not always
to make people believe a particular falsehood.

It is to make them doubt
whether truth itself can be known.

This is a more durable form of control.

Because it does not require agreement—
only uncertainty.

And when people no longer believe truth is knowable,
nothing requires action.

Without accountability,
power stops meeting resistance.

The most dangerous stage of this pattern
is normalization.

People begin saying things like:

We will never know what really happened.
Everyone lies.
Both sides manipulate video.
You can't trust anything anymore.

Those statements sound cautious.
Measured.
Reasonable.

But over time,
they produce disengagement.

And disengagement
is what allows patterns to continue.

That is where the lesson of
Edward R. Murrow
becomes urgent.

Murrow acted in a time
when evidence still mattered—
when people could still be shaken awake
by seeing reality presented plainly.

His intervention worked
because the public still shared
one foundational belief:

Truth exists,
and it matters.

Today, even when evidence is abundant,
repeated,
and verified,
people are being trained to reject it reflexively—
not because it is false,
but because accepting it
would require moral reckoning.

If nothing is certain,
nothing is actionable.

If nothing is provable,
nothing is punishable.

If nothing is real,
nothing is wrong.

That is the final insulation of power.

When seeing no longer matters,

authority no longer needs persuasion.

It only needs direction.

History is unambiguous
about where this leads.

Societies do not survive
the loss of shared reality.

They fragment.
Radicalize.
Harden.

Violence becomes easier
because nothing restrains it.

The most dangerous sentence
in such moments
is not shouted from a podium.

It is said casually—
and repeated often:

You can't believe anything you see anymore.

Once that sentence takes hold,
evidence stops functioning.

And when evidence stops functioning,
accountability begins to disappear.

History asks only one question
at that point:

Did anyone intervene

before reality itself slipped beyond reach?

To understand why these patterns return
at the level of nations,
I have to show
where I first learned them—
inside a home shaped by survival,
silence,
and inherited fear.

What follows is not a detour from history.

It is the place
where history first entered me.

5

WHEN THE PAST
STOOD UP INSIDE ME

I used to believe my parents' past was behind me.

That what they lived through
was sealed in another lifetime,
another continent,
another world.

That what they survived
had already delivered its lesson—
and that history had absorbed it.

I don't believe that anymore.

The moment that changed everything wasn't dramatic.

There were no sirens.
No explosions.
No breaking news alert announcing,
"You know history is repeating itself."

It was just a sentence I heard on television—

spoken loudly, with anger,
like it had been waiting to be said.

A man at a microphone shouted
that some people "were never meant to belong here."

Not whispered.
Not implied.
Said openly.

And the crowd roared.

At first, nothing happened.

It was just another clip.
Another voice.
Another moment in a cycle of noise
I had learned to tune out.

But something didn't pass through me
the way it usually did.

It stayed.

Not as a thought.
Not as an opinion.

As a feeling I couldn't place.

There was a delay
between hearing it
and understanding why it unsettled me.

A kind of internal hesitation.

As if something inside me recognized it
before I did

and was waiting for me to catch up.

That's when I stopped watching the news.

Not because I had decided anything.
Because I couldn't keep watching.

Something had shifted.

I was no longer looking at a screen.

I was watching the past
walk back into the room.

My parents heard almost the same words.

Not on television.
Not in clips.
Not framed as opinion.

But spoken out loud.
With certainty.
With permission.

They lived long enough
to see what those words lead to.

And in that moment,
without thinking,
I knew something they had known
long before I was born:

Sentences like that
don't stay sentences.

That's when I felt it—the shift within me.

It wasn't intellectual.
It wasn't political.
It wasn't even fully conscious.

It was recognition without language.

The part of me that came from my father
woke up first—
the young man who survived
in the forests of Poland,
who learned to measure danger
before there were words for it.

Not fear.
Not panic.

Awareness.

A scanning of the environment
that happens before thought
has time to organize itself.

Then something else surfaced.

The part of me shaped by my mother—
the young girl who learned
that safety can disappear without warning,
that trust is fragile,
that danger can arrive
wearing a familiar face.

Two different survivals.
Two different instincts.

Both alive in me.
Both responding

to something I had just heard—
before I could explain why.

And then something in me stood up.

Not physically.
Internally.

The part of me born
from what they never said.

And I heard myself think—

not as an American,
not as a voter,
not as someone watching the news,
but as the child of two people
who had already lived through
the moment when ordinary life
turned into something
that could no longer be called normal:

This has happened before.

The words came fully formed.

Without effort.
Without analysis.

Not in the same country.
Not in the same language.
Not with the same flags or slogans.

But with the same pattern.
The same tone.
The same certainty.
The same willingness

to say something out loud
that once would have stayed unspoken.

I grew up in a house
where nothing was said,
but everything was felt.

No one sat me down
and explained what my parents had lived through.

No one said,
"This is what happened."

No one explained
why certain things were never discussed,
why certain emotions filled the room
without ever being named.

But I learned it anyway.

Through silence.
Through tension.
Through a kind of emotional gravity
that pulled everything inward.

And in our house, there were things
too heavy to bring into words.

I learned that some things were too heavy to be spoken.

I learned that what isn't said
can shape a life
just as much as what is.

So when I heard that sentence on television,
it didn't feel like information.

It felt like something familiar.

Not something I remembered.
Something I recognized.

And the recognition didn't come from my mind.

It came from what I had absorbed
long before I had language for it.

I didn't feel like an adult
reacting to a moment in the news.

I felt like the child
of two people
who had already lived through
what happens when words like that
begin to circulate freely.

The distance I had always felt
between their world and mine—
the belief that what they lived through
belonged to history,
not to me—
gave way.

It wasn't behind me.
It wasn't over.
It had never been fully gone.

It had been carried.

In them.
And, without my realizing it,
in me.

The day I felt that shift—
when a sentence on a screen
felt like the hand of history
reaching through time—
I finally understood something
I had spent a lifetime circling around:

What I recognize today
feels familiar.

It rises from the same fire
my parents survived.

It never fully disappeared.

It drifted—quietly, invisibly—
into the lives of their children.

Into mine.

And if I want to understand
what I'm feeling now,
I have to go back.

Not to the moment
I heard the words.

To the place
where those words once led.

To the fire they survived.

6

—————

THE WEIGHT OF MEMORY

They were ordinary people
caught in a moment
when the world stopped recognizing ordinary humanity.

History chose them.

My parents were two of millions
thrown into a darkness
no one could fully describe,
and somehow,
they made it out.

What they carried from that fire—
their silence,
their resilience,
their fears—
became the atmosphere of my childhood
and the foundation of this book.

I did not understand, as a child,

that I was living inside a story
that had already begun
before I was born.

I thought every home carried a kind of tension in its walls.

That every family lived with a silence
that could not be broken.

That every parent held something unspoken inside them
that children were expected to feel
rather than question.

I thought this was normal.

I did not know it was trauma.

I did not know it was history still breathing.

No one told me
my parents had survived the Holocaust—
not in words.

They didn't sit me down one day and say,
"This is what happened to us."

Instead, I learned it
by watching the way they moved through the world.

My father's quiet, guarded posture.
My mother's emotional volatility.
The invisible alarms
that went off inside the house
even when nothing was wrong.

My father didn't tell stories.

They sat in his body
the way shrapnel sits under the skin—
buried,
but never gone.

He had seen violence so total
that speech felt inadequate to contain it.

So he chose silence as his language,
because he could not afford
to remember out loud.

My mother remembered out loud
even when she wasn't speaking.

Her pain didn't hide.

It leaked into the way she looked at the world,
into the way she reacted to small things
as if they were immensities,
into the way love never felt safe,
even when it was offered.

She was alive.
But she never fully lived.

I did not understand that as a child.

I only knew that something was damaged—
and no one was going to name what it was.

That is how the second generation learns history—
not from books,
but from emotional weather.

Other children learned family stories.

I learned the temperature of silence.

I learned to read fear
the way other kids learned to read fairy tales.

I learned that something had happened—
but it was too large,
too terrible,
too pervasive
to be named.

I did not inherit the camps.

I inherited the aftershock.

I did not inherit the hunger.

I inherited the emptiness.

I did not inherit the war.

I inherited the belief
that it could begin again
at any moment.

You don't grow up thinking the world is safe
when you are raised by people
who know it isn't.

Nothing in our home ever said,
"You are in danger."

Yet everything in our home
taught me not to trust
that I was safe.

It was not spoken.
It was absorbed.

I did not know
that most children didn't worry
about losing everything overnight.

I didn't know
that other parents didn't check the door twice.

That they didn't react to loud knocks
with a spine frozen in place.

That they didn't treat joy
like something temporary—
something the world was always ready to take back.

When you grow up this way,
you don't realize you are living
under the long shadow of atrocity.

You just think
this is what life feels like.

It wasn't until I was older
that I realized
that most people are raised
to expect tomorrow.

I was raised
to be surprised by it.

The world believes trauma ends
when the violence stops.

But it doesn't end.

It moves.

And so the story of my life

did not begin with my birth.

It began with the silence that preceded it—
with two people
who survived by holding their breath
and a child
who learned to live
in the fragile exhale.

I grew up believing
that I was the problem.

That the tension in the house came from me
not being good enough,
quiet enough,
grateful enough,
obedient enough.

Children later realize the thunder existed long before they
heard it.

What I didn't know then
was that I was living with two people
whose nervous systems
never returned from the war.

My father could fix anything mechanical.

But he could not fix
the part of himself that had learned:

"If they hear you,
they can hurt you."

My mother could decorate a room.

But she could not decorate a wound.

Every loss she endured
lived inside every relationship
she tried to build afterward.

I didn't learn this
by reading their history.

I learned it
by becoming it.

For me, it came in fragments.

A joke about the Holocaust—and I froze.
A question about my grandparents—and no words came out.
Someone telling me,
"You're so serious."

That's when I began to understand:

I wasn't being raised in a family.

I was being raised
in the aftermath of catastrophe.

That realization came with grief.

Grief for the parents
who never had a childhood.

Grief for the child
I never got to be.

Other kids' houses had walls that told stories.

Ours did not.

There were almost no photographs.

The few we had were hidden away—
because every face
was a reminder
of someone
who didn't live long enough
to become a memory.

Most children grow up
knowing what they come from.

Children of survivors grow up
knowing what was taken.

And the strangest part is this:

You still love the people who survived,
but you feel the absence
of all the people who didn't—
even though you never met them.

That kind of grief
doesn't arrive all at once.

It settles.

And over time,
it begins to feel like normal.

Until one day,
you begin to understand:

The silence was not emptiness.

It was evidence.

Proof of a world
that once existed so fully

it had to be buried
so it would not destroy
what remained.

It would take me decades
to understand the full shape of that silence.

Decades before I could name it
without feeling like I was breaking something
that had kept my parents alive.

But the truth is this:

Silence protects the ones who lived through it.

It does not protect the ones who come after.

And one day,
you realize
that you are living a story
you never chose.

Carrying grief
you never witnessed.

Being shaped by a past
you were never allowed to name.

Some people inherit wealth.
Some inherit land.
Some inherit heirlooms.

I inherited responsibility.

7

THE VANISHING CHILD

I did not disappear all at once.

I faded.

Not in the dramatic way people imagine—
not in darkness,
not in crisis,
not in some cinematic moment.

It was quieter than that.
More gradual.
More invisible.

No one realizes a child is disappearing
when the child is disappearing in ways
that make life easier for everyone else.

I did not learn to be silent
because I was told to be quiet.

I learned to be silent

because I could feel that speaking
would rupture something fragile—
something barely being held together
by two parents
who had already survived more
than life should ever demand of anyone.

That is how a child erases themselves—
by sensing that existing fully
would cost someone else too much.

It is the quietest kind of vanishing:

the child who learns to survive
by subtracting parts of themselves
that no one ever asked them to lose.

I learned not to cry
because it made my mother unravel.

I learned not to ask questions
because it made my father freeze.

I learned not to show hurt
because there was no room
for more pain in the house.

I learned not to show joy
because joy felt temporary—
dangerous,
something the world
was always ready to take back.

So I disappeared
piece by piece.

First went the child who needed comfort.
Then went the child who needed answers.
Then the child who wanted to feel seen.
Then the child who wanted to feel safe.

Eventually, all that was left
was the child who knew how to exist—
but not how to live.

The war was over.

But we were still living
in wartime conditions—
just without the vocabulary for it.

We mistake inherited survival instincts
for personality.

We think vigilance is maturity.
We think emotional withdrawal is strength.
We think numbness is stability.
We think not needing anything
is independence.

By the time we learn otherwise,
we have already built a life
around the wrong truths.

And by the time we begin to understand
what shaped us this way,
we realize something devastating:

The child we were supposed to be
never got the chance to exist.

The world recognizes the bodies that were lost.

It does not recognize
the childhoods that vanished too.

The world rewards the vanishing child.

Teachers call them responsible.
Relatives call them well-behaved.
Strangers call them polite.
Adults call them
"so mature for their age."

No one realizes
that what looks like maturity
is often a child learning to suppress need
before they have even had the chance to feel it.

There is a certain kind of praise
that feels like proof
you have disappeared well enough
not to be a burden.

"You're so easy."
"You never cause trouble."
"You're so calm."
"You don't ask for much."

I didn't throw tantrums.
I managed myself.

I didn't demand attention.
I made myself low maintenance.

I didn't act out.
I shut down.

And that shutting down

was rewarded,
encouraged,
protected—
because it made life simpler
in an already tense house.

A child who disappears
is easy to live with.

Until the adult they become
struggles to live with themselves.

People see the outcome
and admire it.

They do not see the cost.

They see function.
They do not see loss.

What they call strength
was once adaptation.

What they call independence
was once isolation.

What they call confidence
was once numbness.

What they call being "put together"
was once the determination
not to fall apart.

We did not become strong.

We became what the environment required

in order to survive it.

There is no language
for the life that never had a chance to exist.

There is only the ache
of its absence.

Some people grieve what they lost.

Children of trauma grieve
what they never received.

It took me years to understand
that the reason I didn't know myself
was not that I had failed to develop an identity.

It was that I had learned
to erase myself
before I ever had the chance to become one.

The world saw someone stable.

Inside, there was only someone missing.

But life cannot be fully lived
by someone who was trained to disappear.

At some point,
if you are lucky—
or broken—enough,
you begin to feel
the outline of your absence.

Not all at once.

But in moments.

In a relationship that cannot reach you.
In a joy you cannot feel.
In a sadness you cannot express.
In a hunger you cannot name.
In a life that looks full
but feels hollow.

And if you finally have the courage
to open that door,
you learn the truth:
You did not vanish.

You were made to vanish.

And now you have to decide
whether to stay gone.

8

THE INHERITANCE OF SILENCE

A special kind of silence seeps through the house of survivors.

It has a way of pretending to be nothing.

It sits in a room like air—
invisible,
weightless,
unmeasured—
and yet it shapes everything inside it.

You don't notice it at first.

You breathe it in.
You adapt to it.

You learn its rules
before you ever learn language.

Because silence, in a house like this,
is not empty.

It is structured.

In a survivor's home, silence is not peace.

It is containment.

It is the lid placed on memories too dangerous to open.

It is the space between what happened
and what can never be said.

It is the shield that keeps the parents from collapsing—
and the cage that keeps the children
from ever understanding
why they feel the way they do.

No one sat me down and said,
"This is what happened to us."

But I knew something had.

Not as knowledge.

As feeling.

I knew it in the way my father went quiet
when certain topics came too close.

I knew it in the way my mother reacted
as if small things were enormous.

I knew it in the way fear could enter a room
without a single word being spoken.

And because it is never named,
the child does not recognize it as inherited.

They experience it as identity.

I did not think,
"I am carrying my parents' trauma."

I thought,
"This is who I am."

Anxious.
Watchful.
Careful.
Emotionally contained.

Silence teaches rules
more powerfully than words ever could.

Do not ask.
Do not upset the balance.
Do not make things harder.
Do not bring attention to what is already fragile.

And most of all:

Do not open what has been closed.

So the child learns to live around the silence.

To adjust to it.
To protect it.

Because protecting the silence
feels like protecting the people you love.

Even if it means losing access
to parts of yourself.

And that loyalty comes at a cost.

You begin to feel things

you cannot explain.

You react to situations
that do not justify the intensity.

You carry fear
without knowing what you are afraid of.

You live with emotional echoes
that have no visible source.

And because no one names it,
you assume the problem is you.

In homes like this,
children become interpreters.

They read tone.
They read absence.
They read shifts in mood
the way other children read language.

They learn what is safe.
What is not.
What to say.
What not to say.

And over time,
they become fluent
in something no one ever taught them:

Unspoken reality.

But there is a cost
to understanding everything
without anything being explained.

You lose the ability
to trust your own perception.

Because what you feel
and what is acknowledged
never fully match.

You sense tension.
But no one names it.

You feel fear.
But no one explains it.

You notice patterns.
But no one confirms them.

So you begin to doubt yourself.

And that doubt becomes internal.

Not loud.
Not dramatic.

Quiet.
Persistent.

Something feels off.

But you cannot prove it.

So you assume it must be you.

And when that happens,
something even more important is lost:

Trust.

Not just trust in others.

Trust in self.

That loss follows you.

Into relationships.
Into decisions.
Into moments where clarity should exist
but doesn't.

Because clarity requires language.

And language was never given
to what you experienced.

It moves through behavior.
Through emotion.
Through reaction.
Through silence.

It does not need memory
to continue.

It only needs absence.

And yet—
there comes a moment
when the silence begins to break.

Not because someone explains it.

But because the child—now an adult—
begins to notice the pattern.

Begins to ask questions
that were never allowed.

Begins to connect feelings

to something beyond themselves.

That moment is not relief.

It is disruption.

Because once you see the silence,
you cannot unsee it.

And once you name it,
you can no longer live inside it
the same way.

You cannot change
what was passed down to you.

But you can decide
whether it stops with you.

9

LIVING WHAT WAS
NEVER NAMED

The hardest part about inherited trauma
is not that it exists.

It is that you live it
without knowing you are living it.

There is no moment
when someone tells you,
"This is what happened to you."

There is no clear beginning.

No diagnosis.

No event you can point to and say,
"That is where it started."

There is only a life
that never quite feels like it fits.

From the outside,

everything can look normal.

Even successful.

A career.
A family.
Responsibilities handled.
Problems solved.

But inside,
something does not settle.

Not dramatically.
Not constantly.

But persistently.

A sense that you are managing life
more than living it.

You learn how to perform stability
before you ever experience it.

You become reliable.
Capable.
Dependable.
The one people count on.

Because you had to be.

Because early in life,
you learned that emotional unpredictability
had consequences.

So you adapted.

You anticipated.
You adjusted.
You prevented.

You learned how to read situations
before they escalated.

How to manage people
before conflict emerged.

How to keep things steady
even when nothing inside you felt steady.

You do not relax.

You monitor.

You do not trust easily.

You assess.

You do not feel freely.

You regulate.

And over time,
you begin to notice something unsettling:

You can handle almost anything—
except being fully present
in your own life.

Relationships become complicated.

Not because you do not care—
but because you do.

Deeply.

But caring does not come with ease.

It comes with caution.

You want closeness.

But closeness requires exposure.

And exposure, early in life,
never felt safe.

So you move toward people—
then pull back.

You give—
but struggle to receive.

You listen—
but rarely feel understood.

You are there for others—
but do not know how to let others be there for you.

The child who learned not to need
becomes the adult who cannot access need.

And because it has always been this way,
it does not feel like something that can change.

It feels like truth.

Work becomes another place
where the pattern plays out.

You take responsibility.
You go beyond what is required.
You solve problems others avoid.

Not just because you are capable—
but because you are uncomfortable
when things feel unstable.

You become the person
who holds everything together.

And people respect that.

They rely on it.
They reward it.

But inside,
it comes with a cost.

Because holding everything together
means you are always holding something.

Always carrying.
Always managing.
Always preventing what might go wrong.

And eventually,
you begin to feel something you cannot easily explain:

Exhaustion
that rest does not fix.

Because the exhaustion
is not physical.

It is the weight
of never putting anything down.

There are other moments.

Quieter ones.

Moments where life should feel full—
but doesn't.

A celebration
where you cannot access excitement.

A success
that feels flat.

A connection
that does not reach you the way it should.

The system learned early
that feeling too much was dangerous.

So it reduced feeling altogether.

And even when the danger is gone,
the system does not automatically reset.

So joy becomes muted.
Excitement becomes distant.

Even happiness
feels like something observed
more than experienced.

From the outside,
nothing looks wrong.

From the inside,
something is missing.

And because there is no language for it,
you do what most others do:

You keep going.

You build a life.
You meet expectations.
You function.

And every once in a while,
you ask yourself a question
you cannot quite answer:

Is this what life is supposed to feel like?

It does not come with clarity.

It comes with discomfort.

Because once you ask it,
you begin to notice more.

Patterns.
Reactions.
Limits.

You begin to see that the way you live
is not just who you are—
it is how you adapted.

Because if this is not who you are,
then who are you?

And if these patterns were learned,
can they be unlearned?

This is where many people stop.

Because questioning your identity
feels more dangerous

than continuing to live inside it.

But for some,
something pushes further.

Not because they are ready—
but because staying the same
becomes harder than changing.

That is when the past,
which has been living quietly inside you,
begins to come into focus.

Not as memory.

But as pattern.

And once you see it,
you begin to understand something
that changes everything:

You were not born this way.

You were shaped this way.

And if you were shaped,
then something else becomes possible.

You can reshape.

Not quickly.
Not easily.
Not completely.

But meaningfully.

And for the first time,

seeing your life
not as a series of personal failures—
but as a series of adaptations
that made sense
in a world that no longer exists.

That understanding
does not erase the past.

But it changes your relationship to it.

What I didn't understand for most of my life
was that this wasn't just my story.

It was a pattern.

Not one that begins in history books—
but one that begins in people.

In how we adapt.

In how we learn what is safe to say
and what is not.

In how silence becomes normal
long before anyone calls it that.

And once I began to see it there—
inside a home, inside a family, inside myself—

I started to see it everywhere else.

1 0

WHEN CHAOS BECOMES SILENCE

What is learned in small, private spaces
does not stay there.

The same behaviors—adaptation, silence, self-protection—
appear wherever pressure builds.

The scale changes.
The behavior does not.

Under enough pressure, very different groups often begin to rely on the
same instincts, the same methods, and the same justifications.

The language changes.
The symbols change.
The moral stories change.

The structure does not.

When people feel threatened, they become more certain—more rigid, more reactive, more willing to justify what they would have once questioned.

Fear narrows the field of vision.

Under pressure, people stop asking broader questions.
They stop tolerating ambiguity.
They become less interested in truth than in protection, less interested in reflection than in control.

The first casualty is almost always humility.
The second is restraint.

And something strange begins to happen:

Opposing sides—people who believe they are fighting each other—start behaving in the same ways.

Not because they agree.
Because fear produces the same instincts:

Control.
Simplification.
Moral certainty.
Punishment.

It does not feel like convergence.
It feels like conflict.

But structurally, it is the same pattern repeating itself from both directions.

When both sides begin to treat dissent as betrayal, language as a weapon, and pressure as justification, they may still be enemies on the surface while becoming mirrors underneath.

It never begins with force.

It begins with words:

What can be said.
What cannot be said.
What must be said.

Language starts to narrow.
Meanings harden.
Nuance disappears.
Labels replace understanding.

And once that happens, something deeper shifts:

People stop using language to think.
They start using language to signal—to belong, to protect themselves, to avoid being seen as the wrong kind of person.

That is when speech stops being communication
and becomes compliance.

They repeat phrases not because those phrases clarify anything, but because not repeating them comes to feel risky.

And when language is controlled, behavior follows—often without anyone noticing it happening.

People begin editing themselves before anyone explicitly tells them to.

They learn what questions are safe, what doubts must remain private, and what subjects must be approached only in approved ways.

Much of the control becomes internal.

People discipline themselves.

We are taught to think of chaos as breakdown, as something that needs to be fixed.

But something more uncomfortable is true:

Chaos can become useful.

When everything feels overwhelming, people stop paying attention.

Chaos does not have to persuade you.
It only has to exhaust you.

A population flooded with crisis, outrage, contradiction, and emotional overload becomes easier to manage, not harder.

The exhausted do not organize well.
The confused do not think clearly.

Overwhelmed people retreat into whatever feels immediate, private, and survivable.

And once people are exhausted, they stop asking what is right
and start asking only:

"Who is in charge?"

That is the shift.

A free people asks whether authority is legitimate, restrained, and accountable.
A frightened people asks only whether authority can restore order.

That is the opening every hardening system waits for.

At some point, people begin to withdraw—

not because they do not care,
but because they cannot keep up.

The noise becomes constant.
The conflict never ends.

The truth becomes harder to locate.

So people narrow their world.

They focus on what is in front of them—their work, their family, their survival.

And it feels reasonable.

On a personal level, it often feels like wisdom.

But on a collective level, the effect is dangerous.

Public withdrawal creates public vacancy.

And what follows is clear:

When enough people step back, the space they leave behind does not remain empty.

It gets filled—by louder voices, by stronger claims, by people who are not stepping back.

Silence, at that point, is no longer neutral.

It becomes permission.

That is how imbalance grows—

not because the loudest people become better,
but because the quietest people disappear.

No single moment feels like the turning point.

There is only accumulation.

Systems do not usually change through sudden failure.
They change through gradual accommodation.

By the time the public senses something larger has shifted, the culture has already adjusted to it.

People wait for proof—for someone to declare what they are doing.

But history does not record intentions.

It records outcomes.

By the time outcomes are clear, the pattern is already established.

Patterns expose structure.

This is where it becomes difficult to look.

Because the pattern is not happening somewhere else.

It appears wherever fear replaces thinking
and certainty replaces doubt.

Where people stop asking,
"Is this true?"
and start asking,
"Does this protect us?"

That is the moment the pattern locks in.

When language narrows,
chaos overwhelms,
attention fragments,
silence spreads—

the direction becomes predictable.

Not inevitable.
But predictable.

WHERE THE PATTERN LEADS

By the time we recognize a pattern at the level of a society,
it has already been forming for a long time.

Because it didn't start there.

Patterns don't begin in systems.

They begin in people—
long before anyone calls them patterns.

They begin in how we respond to pressure.

In how we decide what is safe to say
and what is not.

In how we adjust—quietly—
to avoid conflict,
to maintain belonging,
to protect ourselves.

And those adjustments don't stay small.

They accumulate.

They spread.

They become behavior.

And behavior, repeated long enough,
becomes pattern.

It doesn't happen all at once.

It follows a progression—
subtle at first.

Division.

Then silence.

Not because people don't see—
but because speaking begins to cost something.

Silence creates stability.

At least for a while.

And within that silence,
something shifts.

What once felt wrong
becomes something people adjust to.

Normalization doesn't announce itself.

It settles in.

Gradually.

Until the next shift.

Reality begins to fracture.

Not all at once.

But enough that people stop agreeing
on what they are seeing.

And once that happens,
everything else becomes harder to hold.

Trust weakens.

Systems strain.

People withdraw.

Not because they don't care.

Because they no longer believe
their voice will matter.

That is how the pattern progresses.

Not through dramatic moments.

Through small, human decisions—
repeated,
accepted,
and eventually
expected.

Most people believe they are resisting something because they are
expressing it.

They post.
They share.
They circulate outrage.

Their feeds are full.
Their voices are loud—but usually only where it is safe to be heard.

They speak to people who already agree with them, then accuse others of doing nothing.

And when nothing changes, they conclude that no one cares.

That conclusion becomes proof of their own righteousness.

It allows them to feel morally awake without having to ask whether anything they are doing is altering the reality they claim to oppose.

History has seen this moment before.

It is the moment when expression replaces action, when visibility replaces risk, and when comfort replaces commitment.

There is a name for this:

Costless conviction.

The feeling of courage—without sacrifice.

No society has ever changed course that way.

Closed-loop outrage does not threaten power.
It protects it.

It absorbs energy that might otherwise become organization, sacrifice, or action.

It gives people the feeling of engagement while leaving the underlying structure intact.

And exhausted people do not resist.

They manage.

History is filled with people who believed they were resisting—but were not.

But nothing changed.

Because nothing was risked.

Belief comforts you.

Risk changes history.

This is where fear reshapes identity.

They convince themselves that silence is wisdom, that visibility is danger, and that staying unseen is survival.

But history offers little comfort here.

No injustice has ever been reversed because the threatened made themselves smaller.

Silence may protect you for a moment.

It does not change what is happening.

The pattern is consistent:

Slow decline.
Fracture.
Exhaustion.

And rarely—

Reversal.

It begins with behavior.

It happens when enough people decide that comfort is no longer acceptable as the price of stability.

Reversal always costs something.

That is why it almost never happens.

Those with power resist it because it threatens what they have.

Those without power fear it because they have so little left.

And those in the middle cling to costless conviction because it feels safer than exposure.

Societies do not choose reversal easily.

They arrive there late—or not at all.

It requires accepting that words are seen, stored, and remembered.

That speaking carries consequences.

History has always worked that way.

And I write anyway.

Because reversal has never happened without people willing to be seen.

Risk is not separate from the process.

It is the price of it.

And now the question is simple:

What happens next is not decided only by leaders, or systems, or history.

It is also decided by you.

WHEN SYSTEMS STOP HOLDING

By the time these patterns reach systems,
they have already been lived—quietly—by the people inside them.

Every person reading this book has felt some version of it—in the body, in the bank account, in family life, or in the nervous system—even if no one ever gave them language for what was happening.

What changed over the last several decades was not just policy.
Not just economics.
Not just culture.

It was daily life.

This chapter exists to connect patterns we now recognize with consequences we already know, because we know what happens when such patterns go unnamed for too long.

People begin treating systemic change as personal failure.

They adapt privately to what should have been recognized publicly.

There was a time when stability was cumulative.

You worked.
You planned.
You sacrificed.

And over time, life became more secure.

That assumption no longer holds.

Stability is no longer built.

It is defended—every day.

One illness.
One job loss.
One rent increase.
One unexpected expense.

That can be enough to undo years of effort.

People did not suddenly become irresponsible.

The ground shifted beneath them.

Most people adapted.

They told themselves it was temporary or personal or simply the cost of modern life.

Adaptation felt reasonable because the alternative would have been admitting that something larger had changed.

There was a time when owning a modest home was achievable for ordinary people.

That path has largely disappeared.

Today, there is a real housing shortage, especially in entry-level and affordable homes.

But scarcity alone does not explain what people are experiencing.

The rules of the game changed in ways that rewarded panic, opacity, and escalation.

Closed, blind bidding became the norm.

Buyers no longer see competing offers.

They do not know how many bids exist.

They do not know whether they are close or nowhere near.

All they know is that if they lose, another chance may not come soon.

Uncertainty replaces judgment with fear.

People stop bidding what a home is worth.

They start bidding what it takes to win.

They go tens of thousands over asking.

They waive inspections.

They accept risks they cannot really afford.

Housing stops functioning as shelter and begins functioning as pressure.

And when people cannot buy, they rent.

Often from corporate landlords or slumlords extracting as much as possible while reinvesting as little as possible.

Neighborhoods deteriorate.

Repairs are deferred.

Complaints disappear.

Conditions worsen while rents rise.

Housing stops being shelter.

It becomes extraction.

Education once carried a shared promise:

Effort would expand possibility.

College was not risk-free.

But it was not a lifelong trap.

That changed.

Tuition rose far faster than wages.

Student loans replaced opportunity with obligation.

Degrees stopped guaranteeing stability, yet increasingly became mandatory just to compete.

People did exactly what they were told to do.

And were punished for it.

Debt followed them into adulthood and often into middle age.

It narrowed choices, delayed families, and trained an entire generation to treat survival as the baseline rather than growth.

Again, people adapted.

They told themselves this was normal.

Healthcare followed the same pattern.

It shifted from care to billing.

Doctors no longer practice medicine under the conditions they were trained for.

They are buried under rules, coding, denials, and quotas.

Time with patients shrinks.

Burnout rises.

Good doctors leave or emotionally withdraw.

Care still exists.

But every interaction carries risk.

Deductibles.
Copays.
Denied claims.
Unexpected bills.

People delay care because they have learned the system punishes them for needing it.

Mental health care was weakened precisely when it was needed most.

Families were left managing crises they were never equipped to handle.

Pressure built behind closed doors while the official language still described all of this as a system.

Schools once felt like the safest place outside the home.

Now they reflect a society under strain.

This is not simply a slogan problem.

It is a capacity problem.

More people are unable to cope.

There is less support.

More isolation.

More instability.

More eruptions.

Children adapt by internalizing fear.

Parents adapt by living in vigilance.

Educators adapt by burning out.

The system stretches until it no longer holds.

And once schools stop feeling like places of basic safety and continuity, something larger in society has already weakened.

When people could make a living, they did not have to survive in the same ways they do under prolonged strain.

As pressure increased, behavior changed.

Not because people suddenly became worse.

Because conditions became harsher.

Police, who were once seen as part of the community, are now asked to manage mental illness, addiction, homelessness, and social breakdown —without the training, authority, or support to solve any of them.

We created the conditions.

Then blamed the outcomes.

The pattern repeats once you know how to see it.

There was a time when infrastructure was maintained.

Bridges were repaired before they failed.

Steel was painted before it rusted.

Now beams prop up structures that should have been fixed years earlier.

You can still drive across them.

But if you stand underneath them, you understand the truth more clearly than the official language ever admits.

Maintenance does not generate profit.

Extraction does.

As systems pulled back, families absorbed the strain.

Parents support adult children longer.

Adult children support aging parents with fewer resources.

Mental health needs go unmet.

Stress becomes chronic.

The so-called sandwich generation did not choose this role.

It was assigned.

Families absorbed what systems abandoned.

Love replaced policy.

Obligation replaced support.

And because families still cared, the larger withdrawal of support was easier for society to ignore.

As protection disappeared, pressure did not disappear with it.

It moved.

Sideways.

Neighbors became enemies.

Disagreement became disloyalty.

Suspicion replaced trust.

Sustained strain makes everyone defensive.

Fear does not always move upward toward power.

Often it moves outward toward the nearest available target.

That is one reason societies under pressure become more tribal before they become more honest.

Fear replaces trust.

Blame replaces accountability.

This is real.

This is lived.

And these patterns have known consequences.

Recognition is not melodrama.

It is clarity.

Once people see that what they adapted to is not inevitable—and not merely personal failure—a different question becomes possible again:

What did we stop expecting from the systems we depend on?

And that question demands an answer.

13

———

THE AMERICAN DREAM
—WHAT CHANGED

This may feel abstract. It isn't. You've lived inside some version of it.

Most do not say, "The system is breaking me."

They say,
"I'm tired."

They say,
"I must be falling behind."

They assume they missed something everyone else somehow figured out.

They wonder why they are working harder than their parents and feeling less secure.

Why nothing settles.

Why planning the future feels risky instead of hopeful.

They feel it in their bodies first.

The tension that never leaves.

The exhaustion sleep does not fix.
The quiet fear that one event—one illness, one layoff—could unravel
everything.

This is not laziness.
It is not nostalgia.

It is the loss of stability—felt long before it was understood.

The American Dream was not originally an abstraction.

It was a rhythm.

You showed up.
You worked.
You contributed.

And in return, you could reasonably expect:

a job that paid enough to live,
wages that grew over time,
housing you could plan around,
healthcare you could use without fear,
and the ability to raise a family without constant precarity.

Life was never equal for everyone.

It was never pure.

But for many people, stability was real.

And that reality shaped expectations more deeply than any slogan ever
could.

The Dream is not remembered as theory.

They remember it as normal.

And that normal is what disappeared.

Systems do not simply vanish.

Something replaces them.

For decades after World War II, the central question was this:

How do we build an economy that supports stable lives while still growing?

That question assumed investment in people, long-term thinking, and some degree of shared risk.

It reflected a belief—imperfectly lived, but real enough—that economies existed to support social life, not merely financial extraction.

For a while, it worked.

Wages rose.
Jobs lasted.
Stability was real.

Then the question changed.

By the 1970s, the postwar system was working—but not in the way financial power wanted it to.

Profits were strong.

But too much of that profit was being reinvested into workers, benefits, infrastructure, and the future.

The system was still producing obligation along with wealth.

That became the problem.

The goal shifted.

Not: How do we grow the system?
But: How do we extract from it?

Not: How do we build?
But: How do we pull upward?

You can feel the moment this changed.

Loyalty stopped protecting you.
Experience became expensive.
Stability became negotiable.

Nothing had visibly failed.

The system had changed.

The system had a name.

But the name matters less than what it did.

From this point forward, the economy was no longer primarily organized to support people.

It was increasingly organized to extract from them.

Imagine a tooth being pulled.

No repair.
No replacement.
No concern for what comes after.

The tooth is removed.
The damage is left behind.

That is extraction.

Value is taken.
Nothing is restored.

The system continues as if nothing happened.

Extraction did not arrive as one clear doctrine.

It came in pieces.

Tax cuts were called growth.
Layoffs were called efficiency.
Insecurity was called flexibility.

Risk was called personal responsibility.

Each piece sounded reasonable on its own.

Together, they formed a system designed to move value upward while teaching everyone else to accept depletion as realism.

Extraction does not feel like theft at first.

It feels like pressure.
Then strain.
Then exhaustion.

In extractive systems, failure is not personal.
People are drained by them.

Extraction requires constant pressure.

So survival itself became a product.

Healthcare became billing.
Education became debt.
Housing became speculation.
Childcare became a luxury.

The question changed.

Not: Can people afford this?
But: How much can we charge before they break?

Food used to be stable enough that most people did not have to think about it constantly.

Now it is calculated.

Prices rise.
Portions shrink.
Quality drops.

People adapt.

Parents eat less so children can eat.
Workers rely on food banks.
Older adults choose between groceries and medication.

This did not simply happen.

It was made possible.

When wages stopped rising, debt filled the gap.

Debt does not just extract money.

It extracts choices.

People delay change.
Stay in bad situations.
Remain silent.

Debt is not only financial.

It is behavioral.

It teaches fear, passivity, and containment.

As pressure increased, attention shifted.

Outrage.
Conflict.
Endless division.

The targets change.

The pressure does not.

Division protects extraction because people fighting each other rarely organize against the structure exhausting them both.

Every extractive system tends to follow the same arc:

Growth.
Concentration.
Pressure.
Distraction.
Breakdown.

Then something shifts.

People stop asking, "What's wrong with me?"

And start asking, "Why is this happening everywhere?"

That is the turning point.

Extraction ends the same way it always has:

When enough people recognize the pattern, stop blaming themselves, stop fighting each other, and begin acting together.

That is not sentiment.

It is precedent.

14

———

BEFORE EXTRACTION BEGAN

No one announced that things were changing.

There was no speech.
No memo.
No moment when someone stood up and said, "We are no longer building. We are extracting."

The feeling arrived quietly.

At first, it showed up in the body.

A tension that did not release after work.
A tightness in the chest that followed you home.
Sleep that no longer restored anything.

People did not say, "Something is wrong with the system."

They said:
"I'm just tired."
"It's been a stressful quarter."
"Things will settle down after this."

They never did.

There was a time when employees mattered.

Customer satisfaction depended on people who cared.
Quality depended on people who knew what they were doing.
Stability depended on experience.

Institutions once understood something simple: if you take care of people, they take care of the work.

That understanding faded.

People who had built systems, carried institutional memory, and knew how things actually worked became "too expensive."

Experience stopped protecting people.
Loyalty stopped mattering.

And no one could quite explain why.

Extraction does not arrive as cruelty.

It arrives as pressure.

More work.
Fewer resources.
More urgency.
Less clarity.

Projects begin and are never finished.
Plans are announced and then abandoned.
Priorities shift without explanation.

People start holding their breath.

Just enough for the body to notice.

Meetings multiply.

Language turns vague.

Words like efficiency, right-sizing, and flexibility appear everywhere.

Everything sounds reasonable.

That is how the shift hides.

Fear does not usually arrive as panic.

It arrives as caution.

People stop speaking freely.
They stop challenging bad ideas.
They stop asking uncomfortable questions.

Not because they agree.

Because they cannot afford the consequences.

Changing jobs begins to feel dangerous.

People stay where they are because leaving feels riskier than enduring.

That is how extraction keeps people in place.

Long before people have words for what is happening, their bodies respond.

Sleep becomes lighter.
Patience becomes shorter.
Joy becomes harder to reach.

People feel watched even when no one is watching.

They check email compulsively.
They dread calendar notifications.

This is not simply individual anxiety.

It is the physical response to living inside a system that no longer
replenishes what it takes.

Extraction does not care whether work is meaningful.

It cares whether it produces short-term return.

So work starts to feel absurd.

Projects begin, stall, and disappear.
Resources are allocated, then withdrawn.

People are told to care deeply—and then told it does not matter.

Nothing is built long enough to succeed.
Nothing is funded long enough to mature.
Nothing is allowed to fail honestly.

People learn not to invest themselves.

They conserve energy.
They disengage.

At some point, the logic becomes impossible to miss:

We are not in the business of building things anymore.

We are in the business of moving money.

No one needed to say it out loud for it to be true.

Eventually, the system flips.

Instead of asking,
What do people need to do good work?

It starts asking,
How much can we cut before it breaks?

People become costs.
Line items.
Variables to be reduced.

And when things stop working, the blame moves downward.

Too slow.
Too resistant.
Not adaptable enough.

The system never questions itself.

Extraction does not destroy institutions all at once.

It hollows them out.

Maintenance is deferred.
Training disappears.
Experience walks out the door.

Things still function.

Barely.

Until they don't.

When it finally arrives, it looks sudden.

It isn't.

The damage was done quietly—quarter by quarter, decision by decision.

What happened in one institution was happening in others.

That is how it became normal.

People sensed the shift but could not name it.

So they blamed themselves.

Worked harder.
Accepted less.
Endured more.

That is how extraction spreads without resistance.

The cost of extraction is real.

It is creativity that disappears.
Trust that breaks.
Institutions that forget their purpose.
People who stop believing work can mean anything.

By the time the damage is visible, the system that produced it is already gone.

This is the pattern you were meant to miss:

Build.
Stabilize.
Extract.
Hollow.
Collapse.

It has happened before.

It is happening again.

The danger is not only that people felt it.

It is that they were never given the language to understand it together.

15

WHEN TRUTH
BECOMES TREASON

Every collapsing society reaches a moment when the truth stops being an anchor and becomes a threat.

The cost of acknowledging reality becomes higher than the cost of denying it.

That is the moment when truth stops being treated as a public good and begins to feel like an act of rebellion.

It rarely begins with prison cells.
Or banned books.
Or official censorship.

It begins with something more familiar.

Social punishment.

Truth becomes "controversial."
Honesty becomes "extremism."
Questions become "attacks."
Facts become "opinions."

And the people who speak them become "problems."

Most societies do not silence truth first through law.

They silence it through consequence.

Tell the truth—lose friends.
Tell the truth—lose status.
Tell the truth—lose access.
Tell the truth—lose your job, your platform, your place.

And so people learn a lesson more quickly than they admit:

Lies are safer.
Silence is rewarded.
Truth is dangerous.

Once truth becomes dangerous, those who speak it are no longer seen as brave.

They are seen as disloyal—not to morality, not to justice, but to the group.

That is the turning point.

When people are forced to choose between truth and belonging, most will choose belonging.

That is not because they are uniquely wicked.

It is because exile is one of the oldest human fears.

We are social before we are rational.
Tribal before we are ethical.
Emotional before we are brave.

And so history repeats the same pattern:

The truth-tellers are not defeated by argument.

They are isolated by design.

Not disproven—disowned.
Not refuted—erased.

The more isolated they become, the easier it is for the majority to use that isolation as proof that they must be wrong.

Everyone disagrees with you
becomes more powerful than
everyone is afraid to agree with you.

This is how societies criminalize truth without immediately passing a law.

First, they shame it.
Then, they mock it.
Then, they punish it socially.
Then, they restrict it publicly.
Then, they erase it historically.

By the time truth is formally prohibited, it has often already become unthinkable in ordinary life.

Because the real censorship happens first in the mind.

The goal is not merely to silence the truth-teller.

The goal is to convince the public that truth itself no longer matters.

Once people stop believing truth matters, the lie no longer needs to be defended.

It simply becomes the environment.

One of the easiest ways to stop people from telling the truth is to redefine truth as harm.

Once a society decides that certain truths are "dangerous," "offensive," "divisive," "disrespectful," or "a threat to public order," it no longer needs law to suppress them.

It uses shame.

Truth is now framed as toxic.
Silence is framed as maturity.
Obedience is framed as morality.

This is the moment when honesty becomes "hate" and denial becomes "healing."

People stop speaking not because they no longer see clearly, but because they have been trained to feel guilty for saying what they see.

That is how truth becomes treason.

Not legally at first.

Socially.

You do not need a dictator to punish truth.

You only need a society that confuses comfort with safety.

Once truth threatens identity, the group no longer asks whether it is true.

It asks whether it protects the tribe.

At that point, independent thinking itself becomes dangerous.

Because independent thinking breaks the spell.

That is why every authoritarian culture begins with the same emotional logic:

If you are not with us, you are against us.

Once that sentence becomes normal, truth itself starts to feel like betrayal.

The whistleblower becomes a traitor.
The journalist exposing corruption becomes ammunition for the enemy.
The citizen demanding accountability becomes disloyal.

And slowly, truth is replaced by loyalty.

Not loyalty to values.

Loyalty to a side.

It sounds different. It works the same.

Both the left and the right often believe they are defending truth.

Both believe the other side is the enemy of truth.
Both believe they are protecting the future.
Both increasingly use the same methods to police narrative.

They shame dissent.
They test loyalty.
They punish deviation.
They rewrite reality to protect their side.

The language differs.

The structure does not.

One side may call truth unpatriotic.
The other may call truth harmful.

One accuses people of betrayal.
The other accuses them of cruelty.

Different slogans.

Same mechanism.

Truth is allowed only if it protects the narrative.

Once that happens, morality becomes conditional.

You can justify almost anything if it serves the group.

The enemy no longer has to be answered, only neutralized.

At that point, truth is no longer a standard outside power.

It is simply one more weapon inside struggle.

And that is how societies harden.

Not all at once.

Through justification.
Through fear.
Through belonging.

Through the gradual decision that being right matters more than being honest.

That is when truth becomes treason.

And when that happens, history is no longer asking whether a society is free.

It is asking how much of its freedom it has already surrendered without admitting it.

16

THE AGE OF
MANUFACTURED ENEMIES

When truth begins to lose its place, something replaces it.

Every collapsing society eventually reaches the same point:

People know something is wrong,
but they do not know who is responsible.

And when people are afraid, angry, humiliated, or confused, they will
accept almost any answer—
as long as it gives them someone to blame.

That is when the oldest political strategy in history reappears:

If you cannot fix suffering, redirect it.
If you cannot earn trust, redirect fear.
If you cannot unite the people, unite them against an enemy.

Enemies are not found.

They are made.

It does not feel like manipulation.

It feels like clarity.

A confusing world suddenly feels understandable.

Pain that had no clear source now seems to have a direction.

And that direction feels like relief.

Because nothing strengthens power faster than a frightened population convinced that its survival depends on eliminating a threat chosen for it.

Every empire, dictatorship, and extremist movement has used the same formula:

Identify a group that cannot or will not fight back.
Cast them as the cause of the nation's problems.
Repeat the lie until it becomes common sense.
Turn the public into enforcers of the story.
Let the people police each other.

No army required.

Once a society believes the enemy is internal rather than external, people stop questioning power

and start attacking each other.

That is the moment the powerful become untouchable.

Because the public is too busy hating the wrong target.

It has worked across time and place—because the mechanism doesn't change.

Different centuries.
Different languages.

Same mechanism.

The setting changes.
The language changes.

The symbols change.

But the emotional experience does not.

Fear feels the same.
Blame feels the same.

And the relief of having an answer—any answer—feels the same.

When people suffer, leaders have two choices:

Solve the problem.
Or find someone to blame for it.

Solving the problem requires courage, competence, sacrifice, and patience.

Blaming someone else requires only propaganda.

History is clear about which path most leaders choose.

The Jews of Europe were not the cause of plague, recession, war, or national failure.

But they were available.

Different enough to be isolated.
Familiar enough to be recognized.
Powerless enough to be sacrificed.

That is how a population becomes a shield for those in power.

The persecuted are rarely chosen because they are dangerous.

They are chosen because they are useful.

And once the lie works, it never goes out of style.

Replace "Jew" with whatever label is convenient now:

immigrant,

refugee,
outsider,
elitist,
conservative,
liberal,
socialist,
foreigner,
nationalist,
globalist—

the label changes.

The function does not.

You are not suffering because the system is broken.

You are suffering because they exist.

That sentence removes complexity.

It replaces systems with people.
It replaces uncertainty with certainty.
It replaces responsibility with blame.

And that is why it spreads so easily.

That is how history repeats—

in the psychology of blame.

And the more divided a society becomes, the easier it is to convince
people that someone else is why their lives are not what they should be.

That is a vulnerability in human design.

Manufactured enemies are the easiest and most reliable political tool
ever invented because they solve three problems at once:

They explain suffering without solving it.
They redirect anger away from power.
They turn the population into a self-policing army.

Once the public believes the threat comes from within, you no longer need soldiers.

You have neighbors.

Fear becomes fuel.
Division becomes policy.
Hatred becomes belonging.

And unity becomes dangerous.

Because the moment people stop seeing each other as enemies, they might start seeing who is actually benefiting from the chaos.

That is why every authoritarian movement follows the same unspoken rule:

Never let the people hate the system.

Teach them to hate each other instead.

If people unite, they become powerful.

If they remain divided, they become predictable.

Useful.
Profitable.

Nothing terrifies power more than a population that realizes the real problem is not each other,

but the structure trapping them both.

That is why solutions are never the priority.

Conflict keeps people emotional instead of analytical.

Emotional people do not organize.
They react.

Reaction replaces thought.

They retaliate.

And retaliation keeps the cycle alive.

As long as two sides hate each other, no one notices that the same hands are tightening the same rope around both their throats.

Different beliefs.

Same rope.

Most people inside this pattern do not feel manipulated.

They feel justified.
They feel aware.
They feel like they are finally seeing clearly.

That is what makes the pattern so difficult to interrupt.

The Germans of the 1930s did not wake up one morning convinced Jews were the enemy.

They were taught to believe it.

Not with evidence.
With repetition.

Not with facts.
With fear.

Not with truth.
With humiliation.

They needed someone to blame for inflation, unemployment, military defeat, national shame, and loss of identity.

Sound familiar?

Because if people ever reached the conclusion

Maybe it is not them.

Maybe it is the people in charge.

the structure of power would begin to shake.

So instead of accountability, they were given an enemy.

A target that could not defend itself.

And once a nation bonds over hatred, almost nothing unites it more than the promise of removing the problem.

That is how genocide becomes logical to ordinary people.

They are convinced that evil lives inside someone else's skin.

As long as there is someone to blame, no one has to face the harder truth:

We are being managed.

Turned against each other so we never turn toward the real source of suffering.

The enemy can change.

The strategy does not.

It does not matter who is targeted.

It matters that someone is.

Once the story takes hold, proof no longer matters.

Only repetition.

And once the public absorbs the lie, they begin defending it themselves.

Not because they are stupid.
Not because they are uniquely cruel.

Because believing the lie feels easier than accepting the truth:

No one is coming to fix this.
There is no rescue plan.

The system is working exactly as designed—
just not for you.

That realization is unbearable for many people.

So they choose the relief of blame
instead of the pain of awareness.

That is why societies turn against each other when they most need unity.

Unity requires courage.

Blame only requires anger.

And anger is cheap.

My parents saw this mechanism with terrifying clarity.

My mother lived it when neighbors who once traded bread and
conversation began to look at her family as if they were poison.

Not because she had changed.

Because someone told them she was the obstacle to their future.

My father saw it in the look people gave him when they decided he was
no longer a person,

but a problem.

Jews were not hated because they were dangerous.

They were hated because those in power needed a distraction that spoke
Yiddish.

The same mechanism is operating now.

The Jews of Europe were not the first manufactured enemy, and they
will not be the last.

They were the catastrophic example of what happens when the lie
succeeds completely.

Once a population accepts the idea that everything would be better if not for them,
cruelty becomes patriotism.
Silence becomes safety.
Killing becomes cleansing.

People believe they are saving themselves.

That is the horror of history:

Evil is rarely committed by people who think of themselves as evil.

It is committed by frightened people convinced they are doing something necessary.

Once a society accepts the logic of elimination—physical, political, cultural, or digital—it has already begun.

At that point, there is no longer an "other side."

There is only the enemy
and the righteous.

And once righteousness fuses with hatred, almost anything can be justified.

The strategy works because it infects the imagination before it infects reality.

People begin to see enemies in every disagreement—

every opinion,
every vote,
every neighbor,
every relative,
every stranger who thinks differently.

And once people stop assuming good faith in one another, they become easy to control.

Because people who no longer trust each other will beg for protection.

And power will always offer protection from the threat it invented.

The scapegoat is chosen because they cannot win.

Jews in 1930s Poland did not have armies, political parties, or the power assigned to them by fantasy.

They had bakeries.
They had shops.
They had newspapers.
They had children.
They had neighbors.

But they did not have power.

And when a society is collapsing, the most dangerous place to stand is between the people and the story they have been promised.

Once the public believes its future depends on eliminating the enemy, everything once unthinkable begins to feel inevitable.

Cruelty starts to look like self-defense.

That is why the lesson of the Holocaust is not only "Never Again."

It is a warning about the process that makes "Again" possible.

The world recognizes atrocity at the end.

It almost never recognizes the logic at the beginning.

The beginning always sounds reasonable:

We have to protect the country.
We have to stop the radicals.
We have to defend our way of life.
We have to remove the threat.
We have to do what is necessary.

Those are the sentences that build graves.

And the tragedy is not only that people believe them.

It is that they believe them together.

A lie shared loudly enough becomes a community.

And a community built on fear becomes dangerous.

Not because it is right.

Because it is united.

The modern difference is speed.

What once took years now takes hours.

A message appears.
A reaction forms.
A conclusion settles.

And by the time anyone asks if it is true,
it already feels true.

In 1930, the lie traveled by pamphlet, rally, and speech—slowly enough
that some people had time to resist.

Today, the lie travels instantly.

Algorithms amplify outrage because outrage keeps attention.

Platforms reward certainty because certainty keeps engagement.

Memes compress argument into emotion.

Hatred no longer needs to be taught across generations.

It can spread in a day.

A neighbor can become an enemy between breakfast and lunch.
A rumor can become a verdict before dinner.
A verdict can become policy before anyone has time to breathe.

The machinery is more efficient now.

But the machine alone is not enough.

It still needs fuel.

And the fuel is always the same:

fear and grievance.

Economic dislocation.
Cultural change.
Demographic anxiety.
Status loss.

These conditions make people hungry for a simple explanation.

They want meaning where there is chaos.

They want someone to blame for the feeling that their lives have slipped out of their control.

Those needs are human.

They are not excuses.

What makes them dangerous is when leaders—political, media, or economic—convert that hunger into loyalty.

That is why manufactured enemies are so useful.

They create visible action.

Someone to punish.
Someone to target.
Someone to rally against.

And they hide the harder work behind the theater of blame.

Because rebuilding is slow.

Raging is fast.

Repair is difficult.

Hatred feels immediate.

Righteous anger feels like action.

It gives people identity and instant feedback.

It saves them from the slower, harder labor of civic life:

organizing,
listening,
learning,
building,
sharing sacrifice.

That is why the pattern feels so normal from the inside.

When neighbors, relatives, coworkers, and communities adopt the story, resisting it begins to feel socially dangerous.

The cost of telling the truth rises.

Not only through law.

Through exile.
Through ridicule.
Through lost relationships, lost opportunities, lost standing.

That cost matters because human beings are social creatures.

Ostracism is one of the oldest punishments there is.

And it still works.

That is why so many good people stay quiet.

My parents' generation felt the fists of the state, but they also felt something quieter first:

Their neighbors stepping back.
The shopkeeper averting his eyes.
The baker no longer serving the familiar customer.

The friend who stopped speaking.

Those are the early signs.

Quiet.
Ordinary.
Deadly.

Nothing about it feels like history.

It feels like distance.

Like something slightly off.

And that is why it is missed.

So how does it stop?

It stops when people refuse to let their identity be defined by who they are told to hate.

That sounds simple.

It is not.

It requires rebuilding common ground.
Rebuilding institutions.
Restoring dignity in places that feel abandoned.
Choosing complexity over the easy story.

And it requires ordinary moral courage:

the courage to ask questions while everyone else is shouting,
the courage to listen to a neighbor when the headline tells you to hate them,
the courage to choose real civic work over emotional performance.

There is no magic answer.

There is only the accumulation of small acts that refuse the lie.

Listening.
Inviting.
Working together.
Refusing to reduce people to symbols.

Those are the habits that weaken the machinery of manufactured enemies.

If my parents' generation taught us anything, it is this:

Survival without memory is not victory.

Memory without action is not enough.

We must remember.

And we must act.

Because the strategy of manufactured enemies depends on our willingness to be manipulated.

The most effective resistance is refusal.

Refusal to accept the story that someone else's existence explains your pain.

Refusal to trade your neighbor's humanity for a moment of certainty.

That refusal is not naive.

It is one of the few forms of patriotism that lasts.

17

THE BREAKDOWN
OF SHARED REALITY

A society begins to fall apart when people no longer believe anything
can be proven.

Once truth becomes preference,
once facts become optional,
once reality becomes a collection of "versions,"
a nation loses the one thing a democracy cannot survive without:

a shared world.

You can argue about solutions.
You can disagree about values.
You can debate policy, morality, law, justice, economics, culture,
identity—
and still function.

But you cannot debate reality and survive.

Because if nothing is real, nothing can be fixed.

If everything is "your truth" or "my truth,"
then nothing is the truth.

And when nothing is the truth, power no longer answers to facts—
facts answer to power.

That is the end of democracy.

And the beginning of something older:

rule by force, not persuasion
belief by fear, not evidence
loyalty by threat, not trust

A society that abandons truth does not become free.

It becomes ungovernable.

Not because government fails—
because the people no longer stand on the same ground.

A bridge cannot connect realities that no longer share a plane.

This pattern has appeared before, though it is rarely recognized in the moment.

In collapsing societies, truth does not disappear all at once.

It erodes.

Institutions lose credibility.
Media fragments.
Authority becomes suspect.

And gradually, people stop asking what is true
and begin asking what feels true.

By the time the shift is visible, it is already advanced.

The breakdown of shared reality does not feel like an explosion.

It feels like confusion.
Frustration.
Exhaustion.
Arguments that go nowhere.
Conversations that end in rage.
Families that stop speaking because "there's no point."
Citizens who stop voting because "nothing matters."

People replace thinking with certainty—
because certainty feels like sanity.

You've seen how this happens.

Not when lies appear—
but when truth becomes irrelevant.

Modern systems accelerate this process.

Information no longer arrives in a shared sequence.

People are not just consuming different opinions—
they are consuming different realities.

Algorithms reinforce belief.
Contradiction disappears.

And over time, each person's world begins to feel complete, coherent, and confirmed—

even when it is not shared by anyone outside it.

We do not just have a crisis of facts.

We have a crisis of belief.

And belief—not facts—drives behavior.

If a man believes his neighbor is a threat,
it does not matter if it is true.

He will act as if it is.

His belief becomes reality.

That is how democracies implode from the inside:

not through invasion,
not through revolution,
but through fracture.

Once people live in separate worlds,
they cannot share a future.

This is why fact-checking alone cannot repair a society.

Facts require a willingness to accept them.

When that willingness disappears,
correction feels like attack,
and evidence feels like manipulation.

The argument is no longer about truth—
it is about trust.

When truth disappears, it is not ignorance.

It becomes tribal.

Because when facts can no longer settle disputes, identity replaces them.

People stop saying,
"Here is why I believe this."

They start saying,
"People like us believe this."

Truth is no longer discovered.

It is declared.

Evidence stops mattering.

Alignment becomes everything.

You no longer ask, "Is this real?"

You ask, "Whose side does it serve?"

And once truth becomes tribal, everything distorts:

Facts are "biased" if they hurt your side.
Lies are "necessary" if they help your side.
Double standards become morality.
Hypocrisy becomes invisible—as long as it is ours.

This transformation does not require coordination.

It requires repetition.

Language shifts first.
Labels replace arguments.
Complex ideas are reduced to signals of loyalty.

And over time, people begin to recognize each other
not by what they think,
but by what they reject.

When truth serves reality, people can change their minds.

When truth serves identity, changing your mind feels like betrayal.

That is why people cling to beliefs they know are weak—

because the belief is no longer about truth.

It is about belonging.

And the cost of honesty becomes exile.

In environments where belonging is fragile,
agreement becomes currency.
Doubt becomes risk.

And the individual begins to calculate not what is true,
but what is safe to say.

This is the point my parents recognized before most people did.

Before the soldiers.
Before the camps.
Before the roundups.

They saw something deeper:

the truth stopped working.

It did not matter that accusations were false.

Facts were present.

They were simply no longer useful.

Rumor mattered.
Emotion mattered.
The story mattered.

And once truth becomes useless, society is governed by narrative.

The strongest story wins.

This is consistent across history.

When institutions lose legitimacy,
narratives replace them.

Simple stories spread faster than complex truths.

They require less effort, less doubt, less patience.

And in times of instability,
speed becomes more powerful than accuracy.

Narrative gravity pulls everything toward itself.

Once a society accepts a simple story—heroes and villains, "us" and "them"—everything bends to fit it.

Facts bend.
Doubt becomes disloyalty.
Complexity becomes dangerous.

Soon the story no longer needs enforcement.

People enforce it themselves.

That is how fear stops being an emotion—
and becomes a system.

Once internalized, enforcement becomes invisible.

People monitor themselves.
They anticipate reactions.
They adjust language, tone, and even thought
to remain inside the accepted narrative.

Truth requires effort:

patience
humility
revision
discomfort

Lies require none of that.

Only faith.

Truth demands responsibility.

Lies offer righteousness.

And righteousness feels better than responsibility—
especially when life feels unstable.

Periods of uncertainty increase the appeal of certainty.

The more unstable the environment,
the more attractive simple answers become.

And the more attractive simple answers become,
the less tolerance there is for complexity.

That is why people cling to narratives they do not fully believe.

Because letting go means losing identity.

And once identity attaches to belief,
any threat to the belief becomes a threat to the self.

So people defend what they doubt.
Louder.
Harder.

Not because they have proof—
because they have nowhere else to stand.

Here is the lesson history repeats:

People will destroy reality
before they abandon the story that gives them identity.

Once that happens, facts cannot save a nation.

Only character can.

And character is harder to find than answers.

Character is not formed in moments of agreement.

It is revealed in moments of pressure—
when truth carries a cost,
and the individual must decide whether it is still worth holding.

The most dangerous moment is not when people lie.

It is when people know the truth
and no longer believe it matters.

That is when silence takes over.

"Why bother."
"No one listens."
"Everyone believes what they want."
"It's not my job."

That is how reality dies—
not when lies win,
but when truth retreats.

Apathy does not announce itself.

It disguises itself as practicality.
As fatigue.
As self-protection.

But its effect is the same:
it removes resistance.

My parents saw it begin with small sentences:

"It won't affect me."
"That sounds exaggerated."
"There are two sides."
"They must have done something."

By the time people understood, reality had already shifted.

These sentences are not extreme.

That is why they are dangerous.

They normalize distance.
They soften urgency.
They delay response—
until response is no longer possible.

The second generation does not just study this.

We feel it.

The warning does not arrive with violence.

It arrives in the atmosphere—
when truth becomes negotiable,
when lies become patriotic,
when silence becomes safety.

That is when the future changes.

This recognition is not intellectual.

It is instinctive.

A pattern felt before it is fully seen.

Reality does not break when people are lied to.

It happens when people stop defending the truth.

Truth is fragile.

If no one holds it up, gravity does the rest.

And that leaves responsibility.

If truth is no longer shared,
then those who still believe in it must become its guardians.

Not later.

Now.

18

———————

AMERICA HAS BEEN
DIVIDED BEFORE

America has been divided before.

In 1861, we split the country in two and sent brothers to die.
In the 1950s, suspicion became ritual, and neighbors accused neighbors.
In the 1960s, riots, assassinations, and soldiers on campuses made the
edge feel close.

Every time, people said the country would not survive.

And yet—something held.

Even in anger, even in fear, even in violence—
we still believed the country would survive us.

We believed there would be a future we shared.

We believed in a *we*.

That underlying belief functioned as a stabilizing force.

Even when institutions were strained,
even when trust was damaged,

there remained an assumption—sometimes fragile, sometimes unspoken—
that the country itself was larger than the conflict.

That is what has changed.

Past divisions fought over the future of the country.
Today's division fights over who deserves the country.

This shift is not incremental.
It is structural.

It moves conflict from disagreement
to exclusion.

America once divided over:

policy
law
morality
economics
war
race
justice

But we did not divide over whether the other side belonged.

Union and Confederate soldiers killed each other—
but both believed they were fighting for America.

Civil rights leaders and segregationists clashed—
but both assumed the country would continue.

The Vietnam generation split families—
but not the existence of the nation itself.

Even in those moments,
there was still a shared frame of reference—
a belief that the argument existed inside something that would endure.

Today is different.

We are no longer arguing what America should do.
We are arguing who America is for.

That is not political.
It is civilizational.

Because once belonging becomes conditional,
conflict no longer seeks resolution.

It seeks removal.

A nation can survive conflict.

It cannot survive dehumanization.

The danger is not anger.
America has always had anger.

The danger is moral disqualification—
the belief that the other side is not just wrong,
but illegitimate.
Unworthy.
Less human.

This is the threshold that changes everything.

Once crossed,
debate becomes justification,
and opposition becomes threat.

Once that belief takes hold, force feels justified—

because the other side is no longer "us."

That is how it begins.

Not with laws.

With the quiet death of belonging.

And belonging, once removed,
is difficult to restore—
because it depends on recognition,
not agreement.

We used to fight inside the same identity.

Now the fight *is* the identity.

People no longer say,
"I'm an American who disagrees with you."

They say,
"People like you are the problem."

Language reflects this shift before policy does.

It signals not disagreement—
but separation.

My parents' generation saw where that leads.

The Holocaust did not begin with camps.

It began with a sentence:

"They are not us."
"They don't belong."
"They are the threat."

These sentences do not require evidence.

They require acceptance.

Once accepted,
they reshape perception itself.

Once that sentence becomes normal,
everything that follows becomes possible.

Because limits depend on who is included.

And once people are excluded,
limits weaken.

Every society that failed believed it was immune.

Germany had education, culture, science, philosophy—
and still descended into atrocity.

Not all at once.

One belief at a time.

Normalization is gradual.

Each step appears manageable.
Each shift seems temporary.

Until the cumulative effect becomes irreversible.

The old divisions fought over the soul of the nation.

The new divisions remove it.

A nation is not held together by:

laws
borders
courts
flags

It is held together by belief in each other.

Once that disappears, everything else becomes performance.

Institutions can continue to function formally
while losing their underlying meaning.

They operate—
but no longer bind.

A democracy does not die when people stop voting.

It dies when people stop caring whether the other side remains free.

That is the line between disagreement and breakdown.

America has been divided before.

But never like this.

We are no longer arguing policy.

We are arguing personhood.

And once a society reaches that point,
history no longer asks if it will fall—
only how fast,
and whether anyone tried to stop it.

19

FIFTEEN MILLION

There are moments when numbers say what words cannot.

There are more than eight billion people in the world.

Approximately:

2.4 billion Christians.
Two billion Muslims.
And about fifteen million Jews.

A people cut down repeatedly—
just as they began to grow.

It reflects not only birth and death,
but interruption.
Disruption.
Erasure repeated across generations.

And even now—

fifteen million is still too many for some.

That persistence is part of the pattern.

No one explained Jew-hate to me.

I watched survivors—my parents and others—treated not as people who endured genocide, but as inconveniences.

Their suffering did not matter.

Their differences did.

That lesson settled into my body before I had language.

I learned early:

Jews are accepted—conditionally.

If we are quiet.
If we do not take up space.
If we do not demand memory.

Jewish death is expected.
Jewish survival is questioned.

It operates through expectation—
through what is permitted,
and what is not.

Most people in the world have never met a Jew.

Jews exist as an idea—
constructed from stories, sermons, slogans, and now algorithms.

And when a people exist only as an idea, they can be blamed for anything.

That is how a population smaller than many cities is described as "everywhere."

That is how absence becomes control.

That is how hatred survives without contact.

When societies feel overwhelmed, they do not look upward at systems.

They look sideways.

They choose a target:

small enough to isolate
familiar enough to mythologize
visible enough to blame

For centuries, that target has been the Jews.

Not because history taught hatred.
Because history taught it could succeed.

Jews are accused of controlling wealth, governments, media—even
reality itself.

So ask a simple question:

If Jews controlled the world—
would there be only fifteen million of us?

Power does not look like near extinction.

Blaming Jews simplifies a complex world.

It replaces structure with story.
Responsibility with relief.

Even the language hides it.

"Antisemitism" sounds abstract.
Distant.
Clean.

"Jew-hate" is direct.

Too direct.

So the word softens.

And the hatred survives.

Israel exposes something deeper.

It is the only nation born in survival that is still told its survival is illegitimate.

This contradiction reflects a deeper discomfort:

survival that disrupts expectation.

Israel is expected to endure violence quietly.

To absorb death politely.

To defend itself—and apologize for doing so.

Jewish self-defense breaks the historical script.

And breaking the script creates outrage.

October 7 should have produced clarity.

Instead, it produced hesitation.

And everything was reframed through one word:

illegitimate.

Once that word takes hold,
everything becomes negotiable.

Suffering becomes suspect.
Crime becomes contextual.

If Jews had grown like other populations,
there would be hundreds of millions of us.

Instead—

fifteen million.

That number is not abstract.

It is the result of what happens when a pattern is allowed to continue.

Some still want that number to reach zero.

Some say it openly.
Others disguise it as justice.

This is what an echo looks like:

Old intentions.
New language.

The expectation that Jews endure—
but never resist.

And yet—

Jews remain.

Because survival became refusal.

Fifteen million.

That is endurance.

20

THE AGE OF THE BYSTANDER

Every era remembers the villains and the victims.

Almost no one remembers the bystanders—
even though they decide the outcome every time.

History teaches a cruel truth:

Extremists start the fire.
Bystanders let it burn.

There is only choosing who pays for your silence.

In every historical case, the scale of failure has depended less on the
number of extremists

and more on the number of people who chose not to interrupt them.

The people who watched my parents' world unravel did not all cheer.

Most didn't hang flags.
Most didn't throw stones.
Most didn't write laws or pull triggers.

They just lived.

They went to work.
They ate dinner.
They read the paper.

They told themselves,
"It's not my business."

They assumed someone else would act.

This is how responsibility dissolves—
not by denial,
but by distribution.

Those who make it possible do not have to believe in it.

They only have to ignore it.

Most do not see themselves as bystanders.

They see themselves as normal.
Private.
Reasonable.

Staying out of it.

But normality is not neutral.

Normality is the soil.

What a society accepts without reaction
determines what can grow without resistance.

Bystanders don't say, "I approve."

They say:

"I don't want trouble."

"It's not my place."

And the most dangerous sentence:

"Someone else will handle it."

But someone else is always waiting for someone else.

And while everyone waits—
the worst people act.

Delay becomes permission.

Evil does not triumph because it is strong.

The Holocaust did not require millions of killers.

It required millions of bystanders.

Remove enough resistance,
and the system moves without obstruction.

The question is not:

"Would I have hidden someone?"

The question is:

"Would I have spoken when it was still words?"
"Would I have acted when it was still small?"

People wait for dramatic moments.

But decisive moments are never dramatic.

They are small.

And that is why they are missed.

Comfort sets the boundary of action
for most people in most situations.

History is not a record of what people believed.

It is a record of what they were willing to risk.

Social risk becomes a stronger deterrent than moral obligation.

Nothing cruel survives without it.

The bystander does not begin as a collaborator.

They begin by staying out of it.

But staying out always favors the aggressor.

And slowly—
silence becomes participation.

Every system has three groups:

The few who want it.
The many who allow it.
The rest who pretend not to see it.

The first builds it.
The second powers it.
The third ensures it continues.

The tragedy is this:

Most people did not want harm.

They just didn't want disruption.

So they accepted everything—
as long as it didn't cost them.

That is the real danger:

Not extremists—
ordinary people unwilling to be uncomfortable.

Discomfort is the earliest cost of resistance—
and the one most often avoided.

By the time the bystander understands,
the cost is no longer courage.

It is survival.

Afterward, people say:

"We didn't know."

But they knew enough—
to stay quiet.

That is the essence of the bystander:

Neutrality is a luxury paid for by someone else.

21

THE HERO WE IMAGINE AND THE CITIZEN WE REFUSE TO BE

Everyone is brave in hindsight.

Ask anyone, "What would you have done?"

We do not inherit the courage of heroes.

We inherit the excuses of bystanders—explanations that repeat across generations, often without being recognized as such.

We love resistance stories because we meet heroes after they have won— after the danger, after the cost, after the risk is gone.

We do not see them when they were alone, when they were doubted, avoided, or afraid.

Isolation is part of resistance—not an exception to it.

Real resistance is not noble.

It is isolating.

A hero is not a different kind of person.

A hero is a bystander who refused to stay seated—and paid for it.

It is decision.

My father did not become a partisan in a moment.

He reached a point where doing nothing was no longer possible.

That is where courage comes from—not strength, but refusal.

My mother resisted differently.

Not with weapons.

With endurance.

With the refusal to disappear.

That kind of resistance leaves no records—only scars.

Forms of resistance vary, but all carry a cost.

Most people admire bravery—as long as it belongs to the past.

Because in the present, it costs something.

Everyone says, "If it got bad enough, I would act."

It looks ordinary—a comment, a joke, a silence—and then it passes.

That is how people fail.

The moment felt too small.

Thresholds are crossed gradually, not dramatically.

Resistance is not one act.

It is a pattern of choices:

to notice,
to care,
to interrupt.

It is never safe, convenient, or popular.

That is why so few do it.

Courage is only celebrated after it is no longer needed.

The second generation does not live in fantasy.

We live in evidence.

We know what happens when people choose comfort.

We do not get to say, "We didn't know."

The world is not divided into heroes and villains.

It is divided into those who act and those who wait.

No one chooses decline.

They simply do not interrupt it.

The most dangerous sentence is not:

"I support this."

It is:

"I don't want to get involved."

22

THE COST OF LOOKING AWAY

The cost of looking away
is assumed to be paid by the victim.

That is only the first payment.

The real cost comes later—
when silence spreads.

The initial harm is visible.
The extended cost is not.

No society escapes the bill for its indifference.

Delayed consequences compound.

At first, the cost feels small.
Then it accumulates.

Silence becomes inheritance.

What is not spoken does not disappear.

Unresolved experience transfers—
even without explanation.

Emotional environments persist
even when circumstances change.

The house is rebuilt.
The world moves on.

But the air does not clear.

A society that avoids accountability forgets why it must never repeat
itself.

What is not faced publicly
is lived privately.

You do not have to cause harm
to inherit its consequences.

Silence does not erase suffering.

It redistributes it.

That is the final cost.

WE HAVE SEEN THIS BEFORE

Listen to the language.

"Vermin."
"Infestation."
"Contamination."

Talk of blood.
Talk of purity.
Talk of a people who must be removed because they are poisoning the nation from within.

Crowds cheer.

Leaders shout warnings of invasion and decay.

They speak of enemies among us.

They promise protection—if only the nation is cleansed.

This sounds familiar.

It should.

This is the 1930s.

A society under strain.

Economic fear.
Loss of pride.
Resentment searching for someone to blame.

Hatred mobilizes faster than solutions.

Contempt binds people tighter than hope.

And once human beings are described as vermin, empathy becomes optional.

History records such moments clearly.

But wait.

This is not the 1930s.

This is today.

The same words are back.

The same tolerance for intolerance is back.

The same belief that it will go away on its own is back.

Listen again—without the comfort of distance.

Political figures openly use words like vermin and garbage.

They warn of the contamination of our race, our blood, our culture.

They speak of invasion and rot—of people who do not belong.

They shout as they speak.

And tens of millions cheer.

At the same time, people are taken—

by masked agents
with no visible identification

and no warrants shown.

People disappear from workplaces, from streets, from homes.

And again, people cheer.

Because it's the scum.
The invaders.
The garbage.

Yes, we are not yet at genocide.

But history does not begin where it ends.

It begins with language
and with tolerance.

It begins when cruelty stops shocking.

When there was outrage, he slowed.

When there was acceptance, he advanced.

When there was cheering, he accelerated.

Every step that met little or no resistance became permission to go
further.

What shocked people one year
became tolerable the next.

What was tolerable became legal.

What was legal became mandatory.

By the time people said, "This has gone too far,"
the system already knew it would not stop.

Then the symbols changed.

A new flag appeared—a symbol of loyalty, not shared citizenship.

The new flag demanded allegiance.

The leader became inseparable from the symbol.

He always wore it.
He never removed it.

What began as clothing became identity.

Wear it and belong.
Refuse it and explain yourself.

Neutrality turned into "suspicious behavior."

Laws were rewritten.

Enforcement became selective.

Corruption was excused as necessity.

Cruelty stopped being a failure of the system.

It became the system.

Rallies grew.

The leader did not speak.

He screamed.

The crowd shouted back words of elimination:

Elimination became "necessary."

Accusation replaced evidence.

Once accused, people were no longer treated as citizens.

They became targets.

And when it happened, the killers were not condemned.

They were praised—put on stage, thanked.

Violence was no longer the problem.

Violence became proof of loyalty.

Daily life changed.

Civility disappeared.

Anger seeped into ordinary interactions.

Families split into enemies.

Friendships ended.

Allegiance mattered more than blood.

History began to disappear.

Books were banned.
Libraries were purged.
Education was reshaped into loyalty training.

False narratives replaced truth.

People were no longer taught how to think—
only what to repeat.

The wealthy tolerated it because the markets did not punish it
immediately.

The desperate believed because they had lost everything.

They were told their suffering was not random.

Taken by them.

The vermin.
The garbage.

Once pain was given a target,
it stopped asking hard questions.

It began demanding punishment.

And the ones in the middle?

They hid.

"I'll keep my head down."

Silence felt safer.

So the pattern locked in.

The wealthy tolerated.
The desperate believed.
The ones in the middle disappeared.

And the leader gained what mattered most:

Permission.

What is disappointing—but not surprising—is that Jews, of all people, should recognize this pattern.

We have lived it repeatedly since the Roman Empire:

Blood libels.
Ghettos.
Pogroms.
Camps.
Holocaust.

It is why, in a world of more than eight billion people, there are only fifteen million Jews.

And yet some Jews are embracing the same language:

History has never rewarded that belief.

Not once.

Aligning with power has never saved Jews.

Silence has never protected us.

Believing that this time is different has never worked.

If I were to embrace this language—
to chant it, excuse it, benefit from it—
my parents would have seen it as the most unforgivable betrayal of
humanity.

They survived the Holocaust—

not so their child could become part of the fire they barely escaped,
not so their suffering could be twisted into permission for cruelty,
not so survival itself could be used to justify becoming what hunted them.

To help repeat that pattern
would have made their survival tragic rather than meaningful.

I do not get that choice.

If their lives are to mean more than endurance,
if survival is to stand for more than breath drawn after catastrophe,
then speaking is not optional.

Silence has never saved us.

And it never will.

All religions claim that life is sacred.

Until it isn't.

Until power matters more than principle.

Then scripture bends.

Faith becomes costume.

Belief becomes branding.

Symbols replace conscience.

People wear religious signs while cheering cruelty—believing this will
please God.

But no God worthy of worship
has ever been impressed
by obedience purchased at the cost of humanity.

We are not yet at the point of no return.

That matters.

But every day—every week—we are tested.

Each test asks the same question:

"How much more will you allow?"

Turning back never becomes impossible all at once.

It becomes impossible
step by tolerated step.

Believing it can't happen here
is like believing you are such a good driver that you do not need seat
belts.

You may be careful.

You may never have crashed before.

But crashes do not happen because people plan them.

They happen because conditions change faster than reaction time.

Every society that failed believed itself to be immune—

too stable,
too moral,
and too advanced
to lose control.

Each step produces the same consequences it always has.

Each silence authorizes what follows.

It is like watching a movie when you already know the ending.

You recognize the opening scenes.
You see the turning points.
You know where it is headed.

And still, most people remain seated.

Every generation that later said,
"We didn't realize what was happening,"
had already dismissed the warnings as political, exaggerated, ideological,
or alarmist.

24

WARNINGS NO ONE
WANTS TO HEAR

There is a moment in every collapsing society when the people who still believe in the system begin treating the people who no longer do as the problem.

They don't focus on the danger itself—
just the person who dares to point it out.

That is the curse of the witness.

You don't get applause for recognizing the fire before the flames are visible.

You get silence, distance, irritation, or a smile that says, "You're being dramatic."

And then later—after the damage is irreversible—you get the question:

"Why didn't anyone warn us?"

There were always people who saw it coming.

People who knew the sound of boots marching long before they appeared.

People who had already lived through what others still believed was impossible.

People like those of us who were raised in the shadow of ruin and taught to hear danger as clearly as most people hear music.

Warnings are not welcomed.

My parents tried to warn people before the war—not in speeches or meetings, but in whispers, in hurried conversations, in the quiet terror that comes when the air changes and you don't need proof to know something is wrong.

They saw the faces of neighbors shifting into those of strangers.
They heard the new tone in the voice of a policeman.
They felt the heaviness in the streets—the way daily life slowly became a stage for surveillance.

But no one wanted to hear it.

Not the Jews who still believed in Germany or Poland.
Not the ones who said, "We are loyal citizens. We've fought in their wars. This is just politics. It will pass."

They weren't stupid.

They were hopeful.

It shows up in jokes, in slogans, in campaign speeches, in the way a crowd suddenly looks at the "other."

It starts with the normalization of cruelty—
the public rehearsal of hate—
the idea that someone—some group—is a threat simply for existing.

My parents lived through that transition.

I grew up with its echoes inside my body.

So when I hear certain words today, I don't think "politics."

I think "warning signal."

When people talk about "taking the country back," I hear, "Someone is about to be pushed out."

When people cheer the strongman, I hear the silence of the people who once said he would protect them.

And when I speak about it, I get the same responses my parents used to get:

Every generation says the same thing right before it becomes real.

That is how history repeats—the ones who remember are written off as emotional, extreme, or "living in the past."

And their children—people like me—inherit both:

the knowledge of danger
and the knowledge that few will listen.

I used to think the hardest part of being the child of survivors was the trauma.

It isn't.

When you've been raised in the residue of catastrophe, you don't wait for evidence.

You recognize the patterns.

You feel the temperature drop in the room when hate becomes permissible again.

You can tell when people stop being citizens and start being categories.

You know the look on someone's face when they decide you are no longer part of their "we."

It comes from being right too early.

That is the part no one tells you about.

You feel stranded in a world that still believes in a version of safety you no longer have access to.

You see people clapping for their own undoing, trusting leaders who speak in the same poisoned rhythm you were raised to recognize.

And no matter how gently you try to explain it, you are treated as if you're the one who has lost touch with reality.

People hate being reminded that the world is not as stable, safe, or morally anchored as they need it to be.

That is why survivors learned to go quiet.

They knew the cost of speaking.

I've seen it in Jewish life ever since I can remember.

The very people who should understand the fragility of freedom—who should hear echoes of the past in the present—shrug and say, "Don't exaggerate."

Or worse:

"We don't want to sound alarmist. It scares people."

As if silence ever protected the Jews.

As if the world was ever kind to us because we stayed quiet.

There is a deep irony to Jewish history:

Those who lived through catastrophe are often the first to recognize danger—

but the last to be taken seriously.

Even today, you can see it in Jewish organizations, rabbis, donors, and community leaders who warn against "divisiveness" more than they warn against the people who openly fantasize about authoritarian power.

They worry more about upsetting relationships—with politicians, donors, or institutions—than they do about truth.

Survivors knew the truth:

The people who tell you, "You're overreacting," are always the same people who later ask, "Why didn't anyone stop it?"

That's what no one wants to hear:

The warnings fail because they're unwelcome.

To warn is to break the spell.

To interrupt the sleep.

To remind people that the world is not guaranteed to stay the way they like it.

Instead of asking, "How do we stop this?" they ask, "What good does worrying do?"

They don't want the truth.

They want the comfort of pretending it isn't true.

And when that illusion cracks, they blame the person who pointed out the façade.

The burden of the second generation is often seen as inherited trauma.

But the real burden is inherited discernment—the ability to see before others can.

To know that democratic failure always begins with a shrug.
That hate speech always begins as a joke.
That the turning of neighbor against neighbor always starts with "just words."
And that every "It won't happen here" is a lullaby sung by people who have never lived without safety.

My parents lived without it.

I was raised in that shadow.

So no—I cannot un-hear the warnings.

I cannot unknow what happens when silence triumphs.

That is why I speak.

I am morally unable to do otherwise.

The exhaustion is born of repetition—of saying the same truth in different words, to different people, at different times, and watching it dissolve on contact.

You don't burn out from caring.

You burn out from realizing how few people want to understand.

Eventually, you stop trying to persuade.

Not because you've given up—
but because you've learned the law of warnings:

Individuals don't listen until the danger affects them personally, and by then, the damage can't be undone.

I have lived that truth over and over again—in conversations with friends, neighbors, Jews, non-Jews, liberals, conservatives.

When I talk about rising antisemitism, someone says, "Well, both sides have extremists."

When I talk about authoritarian behavior, someone says, "That's just politics."

When I talk about the danger of silence, someone says, "You're being dramatic. America isn't Germany."

They don't realize how familiar those sentences sound to someone raised by people who once said:

"We are citizens, not criminals."
"This is just temporary."
"They wouldn't dare go that far."

25

WHEN MORAL
AUTHORITY WALKS AWAY

Over the last half century, religious affiliation has declined sharply across the United States.

The trend is well documented across multiple surveys.

The percentage of people identifying as Christian has dropped significantly, while the number identifying with no religion has grown rapidly.

Trust in religious leadership has declined across many faiths.

No single denomination defines it.

It is a pattern that appears across institutions when moral authority becomes separated from responsibility.

Religious institutions keep asking why.

And almost without exception, they offer the same answers:

They redesign websites.
They launch branding campaigns.

What they avoid—what they run from, even when they know it—is the real answer:

The loss of trust did not come from the outside.

It came from inside the institutions themselves.

Across faiths, there is a phrase that quietly enables enormous harm:

"I don't want to get involved."

When clergy say this, what they are really saying is:

"I want to avoid conflict."
"I don't want to risk my position."
"I don't want to upset donors, boards, or powerful members."

But clergy are not private citizens.

They are not bystanders.

They are not observers.

They occupy positions of moral authority.

In most professions, a doctor who refuses to see a patient is committing malpractice.

A firefighter who refuses to enter a burning building is removed from duty.

Yet clergy who refuse to confront wrongdoing—who refuse to listen, investigate, or act—often face little or no meaningful consequence.

They are praised for being "above the fray."

They are allowed to forgive themselves without ever making things right.

The most serious harm inside religious institutions rarely begins with dramatic crimes.

It begins with silence.

False accusations are allowed to circulate.

Rumors are repeated but never challenged.

Gossip becomes a tactic—used deliberately to discredit, isolate, or remove people who are inconvenient, outspoken, or threatening to leadership.

Boards close ranks.

Clergy defer.

Investigations are avoided.

"Both sides" language replaces truth.

And the person being harmed is left alone.

Child abuse continues when adults avoid accusing other adults.

Sexual misconduct is minimized to avoid scandal.

Whistleblowers are labeled as troublemakers.

And when the damage becomes undeniable, institutions do not repair it.

They manage it.

People are emotionally broken.

Reputations are destroyed.

Families are torn apart.

Some lose their faith entirely.

And yes—some reach the point of suicide, not out of weakness, but after prolonged abandonment by the very institutions that claimed to care for their souls.

Meanwhile, the leaders who walked away preserve their self-image.

They say:

"I did the best I could."

"It wasn't my place."
"I didn't have all the facts."

They maintain moral superiority while leaving destruction behind them.

Clergy are certified for intellectual knowledge:

theology,
doctrine,
ritual.

They are not certified for:

courage,
accountability,
moral clarity,
protecting the vulnerable when it costs them something.

In many faiths, clergy performance evaluations are discouraged or forbidden outright.

Accountability is framed as hostility.

Oversight is framed as disrespect.

Doctors take an oath.

Lawyers are bound by ethical codes.

Engineers are held accountable for safety failures.

Clergy—entrusted with human lives, trauma, grief, and moral authority—often operate with less accountability than other professions.

I have seen what happens
when people believe they are acting with moral clarity—
and then choose differently
when that clarity demands something of them.

Not in theory.

In real communities.

Where reputation matters.
Where relationships matter.
Where conflict carries consequences.

That is where moral authority is tested.

And too often,
that is where it fails.

I have called out clergy and leaders for abandoning their responsibilities and moral compass.

And now I sit on the outside because I refused to pretend that silence was virtue.

People I once thought of as friends embraced the labels given to me without ever giving the benefit of the doubt.

They abandoned years of relationship for rumors and misinformation.

What happens inside religious institutions reflects a broader pattern.

This is not just a religious problem.

It is a societal pattern.

Institutions hollow out their moral core while preserving their structures.

They prioritize reputation over responsibility, stability over truth, and comfort over justice.

When moral authority becomes performative rather than lived, people leave.

Not because they reject faith.

But because they no longer trust the people who claim to represent it.

No rebranding initiative can bridge this distance.

No campaign can erase the memory of betrayal.

Trust is built slowly—and destroyed quickly.

And once lost, it cannot be demanded back.

Religious institutions are not losing people because they failed to modernize.

They are losing people because they did not act.

WHEN THE UNTHINKABLE BECOMES ORDINARY

That is the lie people still believe—that hatred arrives like a storm.

It doesn't.

It arrives like the weather.

The temperature drops a degree at a time.
The wind shifts.
A chill enters the room—

and people adjust instead of asking why.

Gradual change reduces awareness.

The unthinkable does not begin as horror.

It begins as tolerance.

One insult dismissed as a joke.
One politician "just asking questions."
One moment of silence because no one wants to say,
"This is not normal."

And then life goes on—

except it isn't the same life anymore.

We are living in that shift again.

The slow acceptance of what was once unacceptable.

The rehearsal of cruelty.

There was a time when a Jewish student being chased or beaten on campus would have shattered the illusion of safety.

Now it is called:

"complex,"
"contextual,"
"a climate issue."

The language softened.

The danger hardened.

What shocks me is not the hate.

It is the shrinking capacity for outrage.

I hear:

"It's complicated."

About things that are not complicated.

I see leaders more afraid of conflict than of truth.

And I hear the sentence that signals arrival:

"This is just how things are now."

That is how it begins—

not with hatred too large to ignore,
but small enough to excuse.

People say, "It's only words."

But words are never only words.

Words are rehearsal.
Violence is performance.

And those who wait for the performance are always too late.

History never returns in the same costume.

The slogans change.
The language modernizes.
The justification evolves.

The pattern does not.

It always follows the same arc:

Dehumanize.
Suspect.
Label as a threat.
Punish for "safety."
Blame the victim.

There is a name for this stage:

The before.

The before feels calm.

Institutions still function.
Speech still sounds civil.
Violence is scattered.

People believe the system will hold.

That is what makes it dangerous.

Because by the time people realize they've crossed into the after—

it's already too late.

The majority adjusts faster than the targeted minority—

not because they agree,
but because they don't pay the cost.

So they adapt.
They normalize.
They move on.

And while they adjust—

others absorb the price.

That is when language begins to rot.

Morality becomes "context."

A Jewish student is attacked:

"Tensions are high."

A mob chants for death:

"It's complicated."

A synagogue burns:

"We need dialogue."

It is not that people don't recognize hate.

It is that they recognize it—

and choose not to interrupt their comfort.

Survivors described this moment clearly.

Not terror.
Disorientation.

Not:

"We are being hunted."

But:
"Why is no one reacting?"

You do not lose safety first.

You lose the world's willingness to be shocked by your danger.

We are there again.

When hate no longer hides.
When it is spoken openly.
When it is broadcast, not whispered.

And still people say:

"It will calm down."
"You're overreacting."
"This isn't the 1930s."

They don't understand:

It never looks like the 1930s.

It looks like now.

The unthinkable becomes ordinary
long before it becomes lethal.

Every nation that fell believed that—

not because they were foolish,
but because they felt permanent.

But systems do not save societies.

Culture does.

And culture can rot.

Democracy is not a structure.

It is a habit.

And habits die slowly—

then all at once.

The greatest danger is not ignorance.

It is the belief that we are exempt.

Second-generation survivors do not have that illusion.

We know safety is temporary.
We know belonging can be withdrawn.
We know how fast the line moves between "citizen" and "enemy."

We have heard the most dangerous sentence before:

"We never thought it could happen here."

And we know the correction:

It is always happening somewhere.

The only question is whether you see it in time.

People demand proof.

They don't believe patterns.

They believe consequences.

But by the time consequences are undeniable—

they are irreversible.

Survivors tried to warn before the war.

The world asked for proof.

It got proof—

in ashes.

That is the pattern.

Warnings come early.
Recognition comes late.

And so we warn—

not to be believed immediately,
but so that when the moment comes,
someone can say:

It didn't happen suddenly.

It never does.

27

THE OTHER SIDE OF THE MIRROR

History changes when language gains authority—

when words stop signaling and start commanding.

Violent language is not the end.

It is the beginning of power.

Once language becomes policy, consequences become irreversible.

Policy gives language force.

What begins as rhetoric becomes structure.

What is repeated often enough becomes procedure.

Nations do not fail because leaders become monstrous.

They fail because language erodes boundaries—until nothing feels unacceptable.

This erosion rarely feels sudden.

It feels practical.
Reasonable.

Necessary.

That is what makes it dangerous.

Killing becomes "necessary."
Deaths become "collateral."
People become "abstractions."

Violence becomes administrative.

Process replaces reflection.

Once violence is absorbed into process, moral distance increases.

The act remains the same.

Only the language changes.

At that point, reassurance appears:

"This is how power works."

Yes.

And that should terrify us.

History repeats not because intentions match—

but because behaviors do.

Certainty drives it.

When leaders believe they are unquestionably right, limits disappear.

Dissent becomes disloyalty.
Doubt becomes weakness.

Certainty allows power to stop examining itself.

Modern killing does not require rage.

It requires process.

One identifies a target.
One approves.
One executes.
One records success.

Each step is rational.

No one holds the whole.

Fragmentation reduces responsibility.

Fragmentation also protects conscience.

Each person performs a task without fully carrying the outcome.

Distance removes consequence.

No blood.
No sound.
Only confirmation.

That is how brutality becomes sustainable.

Sustained systems of harm depend on distance—physical, emotional, bureaucratic.

And once it becomes routine, it expands.

This is not conspiracy.

Small permissions gather.
Unchallenged power hardens.
Normal procedures absorb abnormal force.

Temporary powers persist.
Emergency authority hardens.
Oversight fades.

Strong leaders do not dismantle these systems.

They merge with them.

When rhetoric and machinery combine, restraint becomes personal.

And personal restraint does not last.

Systems built on personal restraint eventually fail because they depend on character instead of limits.

They erode through convenience.

Debate feels slow.
Process feels inefficient.
Power concentrates.

And eventually, the question shifts from:

"Should this exist?"

to:

"Who controls it?"

Once existence is accepted, debate narrows.

The structure remains.

At that point, the shift is complete.

Fear turns inward.
Suspicion replaces trust.
Silence becomes survival.

Inward fear is one of the final signs that public life is breaking down.

Legality does not prevent this.

It has never prevented this.

Law can restrain power.

It can also authorize it.

Legality and morality are not the same.

And the cost is not paid by leaders.

It is paid by those sent to act.

Soldiers carry decisions they did not make.
Families carry the aftermath.
Homes reorganize around absence.

The burden of power is always transferred downward.

That is what disappears when violence becomes abstract:

Human consequence becomes invisible to those making decisions.

When power separates from consequence, democracy begins to hollow.

A healthy democracy requires connection between decision and cost.

Once that connection is severed, accountability weakens.

The mirror does not reflect ideology.

It reflects behavior.

The only question left is:

Will we still say—

"This time is different"?

28

WHEN THE VICTIM
BECOMES THE VILLAIN

There is a moment when suffering is no longer denied—
but explained.

Explanation is often the turning point.

Once suffering is acknowledged only to be rationalized, moral reversal
has begun.

Because once the victim is blamed—
there is no limit to what can be justified.

This is one of the oldest reversals in history:

First, the attack.
Then, the explanation.
Then, the blame.

Violence comes first.
Moral permission follows.

Hatred never says:

"We hate."

It says:
"They made us."

Hatred presents itself as reaction.
That is how it disguises choice.
That is how violence becomes virtue.

The pattern is constant:

The Crusaders.
The Church.
The Nazis.

Different eras.
Same justification.

And the story is always the same:
"They caused what we did."

That story has returned.

Jews are attacked—
and the world explains why.

Jews defend themselves—
and the world calls it aggression.

It is how moral responsibility is rearranged.

The formula never changes:

Attack.
Sympathy.
Blame.

And people will do almost anything to avoid guilt.

The most dangerous sentence is not:
"I hate Jews."

It is:
"I don't support violence, but..."

Everything after "but" is permission.

29

WHEN LEADERS
CHOOSE SILENCE

How the people we trusted to protect us traded courage for comfort

"Now is not the right time."
"We don't want to make things worse."
"We have to be careful."
"We need to maintain relationships."

The ones who had platforms, pulpits, and institutions—and still did nothing—until it was too late to do anything.

Jewish leaders who host panels but won't confront lies.
Political leaders who watch democracy erode and calculate how it will affect their polling numbers.

University presidents who defend "free speech" right up until students threaten to silence Jews.

We are suffering from a lack of risk-taking.

And so, the crisis widens—not because the haters grow stronger, but because the people with power grow quieter.

Survivors used to ask a haunting question:
"Where were the leaders when the world was burning?"

Today, that question has returned.

Except now we know the answer:

They were fundraising.
They were issuing statements.
They were waiting for someone else to go first.

You can have money, power, followers, a platform, a title—and still be a nonentity in history.

You can speak endlessly and still say nothing.

You can "stand with the Jewish people" without ever standing up for them.

The silence is strategic.

Jewish organizational leadership today is built on three survival priorities:

1. Don't upset the donors.
2. Don't upset the politicians.
3. Don't upset the interfaith partners.

"Don't give up on the truth" does not appear anywhere on that list.

- They "condemn antisemitism" while refusing to name its source.
- They warn about rising hate while refusing to confront the people spreading it.
- They host panels instead of protecting Jews on campuses and streets.

They will say democracy is sacred—while supporting the people trying to dismantle it.

They will say hate has no place here—as long as the hate comes from their base.

They will tweet condolences—while passing laws that feed the fire.

So, the truth is left without a seat at all.

Faith leaders could be the moral firewall.

But most have built their ministries around peacekeeping, not truth-telling.

They will light candles for the dead—but say nothing for the living.

They will quote scripture—but refuse to challenge the mob.

They will preach justice—as long as justice doesn't push their congregants out the door.

They punish pronouns more aggressively than they punish calls for genocide.

When leaders choose silence, they don't lose relevance.
They lose trust.

And in every era where that trust disappears, one truth re-emerges:

The people must do what the leaders refuse to do.

Not because they want to—
but because no one else will.

But beneath all of the empty gestures is a single fear:

"If I speak the truth, I might lose something."

Lose donors.
Lose votes.
Lose influence.
Lose safety.

Survivors understood something that today's leaders refuse to admit.

The leaders are not coming.

There will be no righteous intervention,
no one with rank or title to step in and fix it.

That is the moment when history changes—
not because leaders act, but because the people stop expecting them to.

30

MY FATHER NEVER
WAITED FOR PERMISSION

If my father had waited for permission, he would have died.

That truth did not come to him in a moment of courage.

It came in the ghetto—
when the world had already decided who was worth saving.

They died because the world knew—
and did nothing.

It was a sentence he understood.

That is when my father understood:

The question was no longer whether he would live.
That possibility was already gone.

The only question left was:
How would he die?

That was when a sled became more than a sled.

A simple wooden sled—
used for firewood, coal, food.

Ordinary.
Invisible.

But beneath the top layer was a hidden compartment.
A false bottom.

One trip at a time, he and his brother smuggled weapons into the
ghetto:

pistols,
rifles,
ammunition.

It looked improvised.
Scarce.
Risky.

Just the quiet transfer of the one thing Jews were never meant to have:

the ability to die fighting.

It was not hope.
It was refusal.

The Partisans were not waiting to be saved.
They were not waiting for armies.

They were preparing for the only thing still under their control:
the terms of their final moments.

My father and his brother chose to leave—
because they refused to walk unarmed into a cattle car.

Leaving meant abandoning family.

Parents.
Relatives.
Friends they had grown up with.

People they loved—
and knew, even in that moment,
they would likely never see again.

It meant carrying the knowledge:

I am alive
because they are not.

It arrived carrying grief—
and guilt.

The kind that follows you.

There is no romance in that.
Only grief—
turned into motion.

It hardened—
into a reason to fight.

Not for glory.
Not for victory.

But for the people
they had left behind.

For the ones
they could not save.

It is walking away from everything you love,

knowing you are leaving it to die—
and choosing to live with that
so that someone, somewhere,
might still be saved.

My father did not tell this story often.
It was a burden.

The world does not want the weight those heroes carried.

His lesson was not a speech.
It was a sentence.

A wounded one:
"If I had waited for permission, I would be dead."

He was describing reality.

Most would have waited—
explained,
reassured.

"It won't come to that."

They always do.

People admire the Partisans now.

In their own time, many called them:
reckless,
extreme,
dangerous.

They stayed silent because they remembered too much.

It settles into the body.

They had walked away from people they loved—
and knew those people would not survive.

That weight does not disappear.

It becomes inheritance.

THE PEOPLE NO ONE BELIEVES
UNTIL IT'S TOO LATE

Every collapsing society reaches a moment
when the truth is visible—
but still unbelievable.

Not because the warning is unclear.
Not because the evidence is weak.

But because the reality being described
is too horrifying to accept.

There is always a dividing line—
in perception.

That line separates those who interpret warning as pattern
from those who dismiss it as exaggeration.

Those who recognize the danger early—
and those who refuse to believe it applies to them.

The first group sees what is coming

while there is still time to stop it.

The second group says:
"You're overreacting."
"You're being emotional."
"You're not helping."

They discipline the person giving it.

And by then, it is too late.

History remembers the victims.
It remembers the villains.

It forgets the people
who tried to stop it
before it began.

The one who warns
is mocked first
and believed last.

I was raised by survivors
who taught something else:

Do not wait for permission to see danger.

And do not expect to be thanked
for noticing it early.

Not just trauma.
Clarity.

DEMOCRACIES DON'T FALL —THEY ARE SURRENDERED

Democracies do not fall the way people imagine.

They are dismantled slowly.
Legally.
Incrementally.

And most of the time,
with the participation of the very people
who believe they are protecting them.

Citizens end democracies—
through delay,
through denial,
through exhaustion,
through the belief
that someone else will stop it.

They end in normalization.

The most dangerous sentence
in any collapsing society is:
"This is still legal."

New laws.
New definitions.
New limits "for safety."
New punishments "for stability."
New enemies "for the good of the country."

And millions of people saying:
"Well... this doesn't affect me."

Paperwork does most of the damage.

The greatest threat to democracy
has never been extremists.

It has always been the majority
that waits too long to act.

And the people who see the danger first
are always called alarmists—
until they are proven right.

Authoritarians do not need universal support.
They only need widespread inaction:

A small group that acts.
A large group that waits.
A targeted group that absorbs the cost.

And a country full of people saying:
"It won't go that far."

That is how democracies are surrendered.

When democracy begins to disappear,
life does not immediately look different.

And most people say:
"If things were really collapsing,
wouldn't it feel worse?"

But this does not feel like chaos
in the beginning.

It feels like stability.
It feels like someone else's problem.

By the time the majority feels it,
the outcome has already been decided.

It falls because of cooperation.

Judges who follow orders.
Police who "enforce the law."
Journalists who normalize what they should expose.
Religious leaders who bless what they should challenge.
Citizens who stay quiet to protect their comfort.
Professionals who say:
"I don't want to get involved."

It is surrendered
through participation.

Authoritarian power is expected
to come through violence.

More often,
it comes through process:

Elections.

Appointments.
Decrees.
Courts.
Legislation.

The tyrant does not need to break the law.
He only needs to control
the people who interpret it.

It will not arrive
in recognizable form.

It will come dressed as:

"Election integrity"
"Law and order"
"Protecting children"
"Defending freedom"
"Restoring greatness"

It will not feel like a takeover.
It will feel like policy.

Books removed "for safety."
Protests restricted "for security."
Journalists investigated "for accountability."
Opponents charged "for corruption."

And those who object
will be labeled:
Un-American.

Democracy does not end
when power is taken.

It ends when people stop believing
their voice matters.

And without participation,
democracy is already gone.

WHEN THE LAW STOPS
PROTECTING YOU

It does not become dangerous
when laws are broken—
but when the law no longer protects
those it was created for
and still demands obedience.

The people who carried out the worst crimes
of the twentieth century did not say:
"I am breaking the law."

They said:
"I am following it."

That is the moment
a democracy crosses the line:

Not when the powerful ignore the law—
but when they control it.

Because once they control the law,

they control the definition of crime.

And once they control the definition of crime,
they control you.

People are taught to trust it.
To respect it.
To rely on it.

But something else is true:

The law has always protected some people
and controlled others.

Legality is power
with paperwork.

People who say,
"It can't happen here,"
are imagining illegal persecution.

But real persecution
almost always arrives legally—
because laws are easier to change
than human conscience.

The real question is not:
"Will the law be broken?"

The real question is:
"Who will the law be written for?"

The system looks the same.
Only the target changes.

It begins with one group.

And then they say it must continue—
because the danger has now been "proven."

And the majority says:
"Well... that doesn't affect me."

You are a category.

You no longer have rights.
You have permissions.

And permissions can be revoked.

You no longer have protection.
You have conditions for protection.

You no longer have equal standing.
You have assigned status.

The lesson is always the same:

Rights are not lost
when they are taken.

They are lost
when enough people believe
they cannot be taken.

34

WHEN COURAGE BECOMES ILLEGAL

Every collapsing society reaches a moment
when the people who act conscientiously
become the ones labeled dangerous.

Not the extremists.
Not the tyrants.
Not the mobs.

But the ones who refuse to obey
what they know is wrong.

There is always a point where the line flips:

Silence becomes "responsible."
Obedience becomes "patriotic."
Compliance becomes "good citizenship."
And resistance—even quiet, nonviolent, moral resistance—becomes a
threat to the state.

Courage becomes punishable.

And the majority goes along every step of the way
because they have already chosen the safer identity:

That sentence—more than bullets, laws, or tyrants—
is what buries democracies.

This shift rarely feels dramatic while it is happening.

It unfolds through language, policy, and social pressure—each step
small enough to justify, each step easy enough to accept.

By the time courage is openly punished,
the culture has already been trained
to see it as a threat rather than a duty.

In the ghetto, the people with the most courage were not
honored.

They were suspected.
They were watched.
They were whispered about.
They were told they would get everyone killed.
They were called reckless.
They were told to be patient.
They were warned not to "provoke" the oppressors.

They were judged by people
who would soon be dead.

And when my father and a handful of others decided,

"We will not wait to be marched to our deaths,"

that decision—to live as a free person,
even for one more day—

was illegal.

Smuggling weapons was illegal.
Organizing escape was illegal.
Joining the Partisans was illegal.
Saying "no" to the Nazis was illegal.

They did it anyway.

Because they refused to surrender
the last human choice left to them:

how they would die.

What made their actions criminal was not the morality of what they did,
but the authority that defined morality itself.

When a system demands obedience to injustice,
the law does not distinguish between right and wrong—

it distinguishes between compliance and resistance.

Authoritarians don't just outlaw courage.

They make people ashamed of it.

The goal is not to kill courage—
but to isolate it.

Once courageous people feel alone,
the battle is nearly over.

Isolation transforms courage into liability.

When people believe they are the only ones willing to act,
resistance begins to feel futile—

not because it is,
but because it appears unsupported.

That perception is often enough
to stop action before it begins.

The ones who:

Speak when silence is demanded.
Defend those already written off.
Reject the new "normal."
Refuse to participate in cruelty.
Stand between power and its target.
Tell the truth after it becomes illegal.

They are not radicals.

They are the last true citizens left.

When the law demands obedience to injustice,

People have to decide who they fear more—

the state
or their own conscience?

Every generation answers that question.

Many fail it.

But someone always has to go first.

And that is the real definition of courage:

Decline does not begin when courage becomes dangerous.

It begins when courage becomes rare.

35

THE LAST ILLUSION—SOMEONE ELSE WILL STOP THIS

People don't surrender their freedoms because they support tyranny.

They lose them because they assume someone else will stop it.

Someone braver.
Someone with power.
Someone with authority.
Someone with a platform.

But "someone" never comes.

In every era, the people who notice the danger early look around
and say:

"I can't fix this.
This is too big.
Someone else has to step in."

They wait for leaders.
The leaders wait for institutions.
The institutions wait for laws.

The laws wait for courts.
The courts wait for elections.

And the crisis advances—uninterrupted.

Responsibility does not disappear when it is deferred.

Each layer that waits transfers the burden downward until no one is left
to act.

By then, the structure that could have resisted has already stalled itself.

Millions of Germans thought Adolf Hitler was temporary.

They assumed:

The generals would stop him.
The churches would stop him.
The constitution would stop him.
The Allies would stop him.

They waited for someone else to act—

and by the time they realized the "someone else" was never coming,
they were afraid to act at all.

What makes this pattern so dangerous is not ignorance, but misplaced
trust.

People believe that institutions will correct what individuals are
unwilling to confront.

When those institutions fail—or choose not to act—
the delay becomes irreversible.

Doing nothing is not passive.

Inaction is not an absence of choice—

it is a decision to accept the outcome created by others.

Silence makes people feel moral.
Delegation makes people feel sane.
Avoidance makes people feel peaceful.

But none of those things make people free.

The world is not destroyed by evil,
but by people waiting for someone else to stop evil.

There is no "someone else."

There is only the one who acts—

and the one who lives with the cost of not acting.

WHAT IT TAKES TO ACT ANYWAY

Seeing clearly is not the hard part.

Most people see more than they admit. They notice when something feels off. They recognize when words no longer match actions. They sense when something is shifting in a direction that does not feel right. That is not rare.

What is rare is acting on it.

Because the moment you move from seeing to saying, everything changes. What was internal becomes visible. And once it is visible, it carries consequences—not always dramatic, not always immediate, but real.

You may not lose everything. But you lose something: certainty, ease, and the sense that you can remain untouched by what is happening around you.

And often, you lose something else: alignment.

Not alignment with truth—alignment with people.

Because the moment you speak when others are still calculating, you step out of sync. You create distance, even if no one says it out loud.

Conversations shift. Interactions tighten. People who once felt close begin to pull back—not abruptly, not obviously, but enough.

This is where most people stop.

Not because they do not care, but because they understand what comes next: distance, tension, and misinterpretation. Sometimes, silence replaces what used to be connection.

So they wait.

They wait for the right time, the right wording, the right support.

But that moment rarely comes.

Because acting is what creates the moment—not the other way around.

What it takes to act anyway is often misunderstood.

It does not require certainty. If you wait for certainty, you will wait forever. It does not require consensus. If you need agreement, you are already too late.

It requires something quieter: a willingness to be out of alignment for a period of time.

To hold your position without immediate reinforcement. To accept that being understood may not happen right away—or at all.

That is the part most people are not prepared for.

We are taught that if something is true, others will eventually recognize it.

Sometimes they do.

But often, they already have—and are still deciding what to do with it.

Which means your action does not create clarity for them.

It creates pressure.

And pressure forces a choice.

That is why the first person to act often absorbs the impact—not because they are wrong, but because they moved first.

To act anyway requires separating two things most people instinctively tie together: truth and outcome.

You may speak the truth and not change the outcome. You may act with clarity and still lose position, relationships, or influence.

If your decision depends on the outcome, you will not act.

But if your decision is anchored in something else—integrity, consistency, a refusal to pretend you do not see what you see—then the outcome becomes secondary. Not irrelevant, but not controlling.

This does not make it easier.

It makes it possible.

Because the real barrier is not fear.

It is attachment.

Attachment to how things are. To how people see you. To where you fit inside the structure.

Letting go of that—even temporarily—is what creates the space to act.

Not perfectly. Not without consequence. But honestly.

And once you do that, something shifts.

Not always externally.

But internally.

You stop negotiating with what you know. You stop adjusting to remain comfortable. And whether others follow or not, you are no longer waiting.

That is the difference.

Most people are waiting.

And in that waiting, patterns continue—not because they are hidden, but because they are tolerated.

Acting does not guarantee change.

But it interrupts what would otherwise continue unchallenged.

That is the role.

Not to control the outcome. Not to force agreement.

But to break the pattern of silence that allows everything else to continue.

That is what it takes.

Not certainty. Not approval.

A willingness to act before those things arrive.

37

THE ONES WHO ACT ANYWAY

In every collapsing society, there is a moment when the majority has already surrendered—through silence, delay, and the belief that someone else will intervene.

And yet, in every era, there is also a small, stubborn, unexplainable group of people who refuse to wait.

What they retain is something the majority has already given away: the refusal to let fear decide who they are.

They are the ones who act anyway.

They are not the majority. They never have been.

It is always the few—not the many—who break the spell first.

A handful of partisans in the forests.
A few families hiding Jews in their attics.
Journalists printing what could get them jailed.
Students standing when everyone else stays seated.
Women saying no before a country remembers what no means.

History is not moved by crowds. Crowds follow.

History is moved by the people who stand up before standing is safe.

What separates these individuals is not strength or certainty, but timing. They act before consensus forms, before protection exists, and before the outcome is clear.

That is why they appear isolated in the moment—and decisive in hindsight.

People like to romanticize resistance, as if it were fueled by heroism.

But most resistance begins with something simpler and more honest: refusal.

My father and the others did not run to the forests because they were fearless. They ran because they understood that the trains were not taking people to work, that no one was coming to save them, and that waiting meant dying on someone else's terms.

So they acted—because living with obedience was worse than dying with defiance.

They did not choose survival. They chose dignity.

Survival followed—for some of them, but not most.

They were not the loudest. They were not the strongest. They were not the most educated, the most armed, or the most supported.

They had only this in common:

They had reached the point where doing nothing cost more than risking everything.

And once they crossed that line, they did not go back.

That threshold—the moment when inaction becomes more costly than action—is the turning point most people avoid.

Those who act are not different in kind. They simply reach that point sooner.

That is why resisters are rarely embraced in real time.

Today, that pattern continues.

Teachers refusing to erase history from classrooms.
Rabbis and pastors who will not choose silence over truth.
Journalists fired for printing what power wants buried.
Women refusing to lose rights their grandmothers had already won.
Immigrants warning, "I have seen this before."

They act because they are done being silent.

The world does not change when everyone is ready.

It changes when enough people decide they no longer need permission.

3 8

OUTRAGE WITHOUT ACTION

Every day I watch people forward articles, repost memes, share warnings,
and tag others in messages like:
"This is terrifying—someone needs to do something."

They sound alarmed.

But they never say what they are doing.

They demand action while practicing avoidance.

This is the new form of surrender.

Clicking is participating.
Posting is resisting.
Anger is accountability.

It is the perfect design for those in power:

Millions of people convinced they are "in the struggle,"
while never once leaving the comfort of the screen.

The government doesn't have to censor anyone
when people willingly limit their activism to the "share" button.

Digital expression creates the feeling of engagement
without requiring commitment.

Too many don't want to fight injustice.

They don't want to participate in resistance.

Digital courage requires only Wi-Fi.

A repost costs nothing.
A meme costs nothing.

The only thing being risked is nothing.

That is why digital outrage is so addictive.

It delivers the emotional reward of activism
without a single consequence.

No lost friendships.
No real threat.
No risk.

Systems do not respond to sentiment alone—
they respond to pressure, disruption, and sustained effort.

Real action is not convenient.
And it is never cost-free.

Real action demands:

Time.
Commitment.
Exposure.
Consequence.

History is not shaped by the people who forward information—
but by the people who refuse to forward responsibility.

Outrage is emotional.
Opposition is strategic.

Outrage reacts.
Opposition interrupts.

A meme has never stopped a fascist.
A hashtag has never stopped a prejudiced law.

And yet millions of people convince themselves they are "in the fight"
because they react to the world instead of confronting it.

They care just enough to feel something—
but not enough to do something.

The future will not be decided by those who feel the most outrage—
but by those who refuse to stop at just outrage.

39

THE PRICE OF DOING NOTHING

The greatest cost in a collapsing society
is assumed to be paid by those who resist.

And yes—they pay a price.

They lose jobs.
They lose status.
They lose safety.

They are attacked, discredited, isolated, and silenced.

That cost is real.

But it is not the greatest cost.

The greatest cost is paid by those who do nothing.

Because doing nothing does not mean avoiding consequences.

It means choosing which consequences you will accept.

You do not stay out of the fight.

You just lose the right to decide
how it ends.

Control is not lost in a single moment.

It is transferred gradually—
from those who could act
to those who are willing to act.

The longer people wait,
the fewer choices remain.

The fewer choices remain,
the higher the cost of action becomes.

Until eventually,
action becomes nearly impossible—
and inaction becomes irreversible.

This is the hidden cost of silence.

It does not protect you.

It conditions you.

It trains you to accept what you once would have resisted.

At first, the changes feel uncomfortable.

Then they feel normal.

Then they feel necessary.

That is how societies transform
without ever declaring that they have changed.

Not through belief—
but through adaptation.

Not through agreement—
but through repetition.

Not through conviction—
but through avoidance.

A person who repeatedly avoids confrontation
does not remain neutral.

They become compliant.

A population that repeatedly chooses comfort over resistance
does not remain stable.

It becomes controllable.

This is how freedom disappears—
not in a dramatic collapse,
but in a series of small surrenders.

One person looks away from cruelty.

Another justifies it.

Another accepts it as normal.

Another teaches their children

to do the same.

And over time,
what once would have been unthinkable
becomes expected.

Doing nothing is not just a personal decision.

It is a generational one.

Because the consequences of inaction

are inherited.

Children do not just inherit the world
their parents built.

They inherit the world
their parents tolerated.

And once that inheritance is set,
it cannot be undone easily.

That is why the cost of inaction
is rarely understood in the moment.

It is paid later—
by people who had no voice in the decision.

Someone always pays for inaction—
but it is rarely the one who chose it.

The final cost
is not just what is lost.

It is the realization
that something could have been done
when it still mattered.

That realization does not arrive as clarity.

It arrives as regret.

And regret is not just sadness.

It is the awareness
that a different outcome was possible—
and that it was allowed to disappear.

By the time that awareness arrives,
the opportunity to act
has already passed.

And no amount of hindsight, apology, or grief
can change a single thing.

40

NO ONE SEES THE
TURNING POINT

No one recognizes the turning point when it happens.

It does not feel like collapse.
It feels ordinary.
It feels manageable.
It feels like "things are bad, but not that bad."
It feels like "we still have time."

The moment the future is decided is never announced as such.

It is presented as stability, safety, order,
or "necessary change."

The people living through it rarely understand its meaning in real time.

They only understand it later—
when the choices that once existed
no longer do.

Turning points are not defined by what happens.

They are defined by how people interpret what is happening.

Every turning point creates two groups of people:

Those who say:
"Calm down. Institutions will hold."

And those who say:
"This is the moment. Act now."

The first group always sounds reasonable.
The second group always sounds extreme.

At the time, the people urging caution are seen as rational.
The people urging action are seen as dangerous.

History reverses those judgments.

The greatest danger is not when people see the fire—
but when they smell smoke
and convince themselves
it is nothing.

Because by the time the fire is visible,
the conditions that allowed it to spread
are already in place.

The tragedy of the turning point
is not that it is hidden.

It is that it is visible—
but interpreted as temporary.

People tell themselves:
"This will pass."
"This has happened before."

"This is not who we are."

But every irreversible change
once looked temporary.

Every system that failed
once looked stable.

Every loss of freedom
once felt like an exception.

That is how societies cross the line
without ever feeling like they crossed it.

They do not wake up in a different world.
They adjust to it—
one decision,
one compromise,
one silence at a time.

By the time the change is undeniable,
it is no longer reversible.

The people who warned early
are no longer dismissed—
but they are also no longer needed.

Because the moment when warning mattered
has already passed.

The question is never whether a turning point exists.

The question is whether people will recognize it
before it becomes permanent.

41

THE LINE THAT STILL EXISTS

There is always a point in every collapsing society
when the people still have enough power
to change the ending—
if they use it before it is taken from them.

That point is never obvious.
It doesn't come with an announcement.

No bell rings.
No headline reads, "Last chance."

It is a narrow, fading line
visible only to those who understand
that inaction itself is a vote.

We are living on that line right now.

It is the belief that once the damage begins,
nothing done afterward matters.

It is never "too late"
until the people who know the danger stop acting.

As long as people can still speak, gather, vote, protest, organize—
the line still exists.

What feels like inevitability is often the result
of people withdrawing from the tools
that still remain available to them.

A broken system can still be fought.
A finished system cannot.

A broken system allows dissent.
A finished one punishes it.

That is why the line must be recognized
before people start adjusting.

People can still speak without being jailed.
People can still gather without permission.
People can still vote.

None of these are guaranteed to last.

They only exist for as long as people use them.

My father did not escape the ghetto when the walls went up.
He escaped when the transports began.

Before that, resistance meant others would die in retaliation.
After that, everyone was already marked for death.

That was the turning point.

Not when danger started—
but when obedience no longer reduced it.

The choice shifted from:

"Who will die if I resist?"

to:

"How will I die if I don't?"

And once obedience could no longer save anyone,
resistance became the last act of dignity.

Every right not used becomes a privilege.
Every privilege not defended becomes a memory.

We are not out of time.

We are out of the illusion that time will fix anything.

The line is still here.
But it is narrowing.

And it will not remain forever.

THE CHOICE THAT
CANNOT BE ESCAPED

Every generation thinks it can delay the moment of decision.

That it can wait for clarity.
That it can stay "neutral" until the danger becomes undeniable.
That it can postpone responsibility until someone else acts first.

But history has no neutral column.

There is no balcony to watch from.

There is no seat reserved for those who "did nothing but meant no harm."

When a society reaches the point we are now living in,
everyone is already choosing—
whether they admit that choice or not.

People imagine collaborators as the ones
who cheer the regime,
wave the flags,
enforce the rules,

and salute the leader.

But most collaboration is quieter.

"This isn't my fight."
"I'm not political."

Those sentences have carried more dictators to power
than armies ever have.

Tyranny does not require millions of believers.

It only requires millions of avoiders.

Collaboration often looks passive,
because it does not always announce itself as loyalty.

More often, it appears as withdrawal, postponement,
and the refusal to oppose what is taking shape.

That is what makes it so common—

and so dangerous.

You can stay silent,

but silence still votes.

People like to say:

"I'm not choosing."

But history replies:

"You already did."

There is always:

A small number actively doing harm.
A larger number being harmed.
And a vast majority calling itself "uninvolved."

But the uninvolved are never uninvolved.

They are the deciding force.

The world is not destroyed by evil alone,
but by the people who let evil organize itself into power.

Majorities often believe that because they are not initiating harm,
they stand outside it.

The opposite is true.

The group that withholds resistance determines
whether the smaller group doing harm remains isolated—
or becomes effective.

My father did not get to choose
whether the world was collapsing.

He only got to choose
how he would live inside the destruction.

That is the real decision.

Not:

Can this be stopped?

But:

What will I become in the face of it?

He did not get to choose safety.

He only got to choose whether he would obey.

He did not get to choose certainty.

He only got to choose whether he would act without it.

That is the same choice we face now.

4 3

BREAKING THE PATTERN

Every era that destroyed itself
believed the pattern was unbreakable.

Every collapsing society told itself the same lie:

This is just the way things are now.

But something else emerges—
something quieter, smaller, and harder to see.

There have been moments
when the pattern did not win.

Not because the danger was less.
Not because the oppressors were weaker.
Not because the people were braver.

The pattern broke
when enough people refused to behave
the way collapsing societies always behave.

The pattern is not a prophecy.

It is a habit.

And habits can be shattered.

The pattern only works
when people behave the same way every time.

Breaking the pattern does not require a miracle.
It requires interruption.

A pattern continues because behavior continues.
Once behavior changes, the inevitability disappears with it.

44

WHAT IT MEANS TO ACT
BEFORE VICTORY IS POSSIBLE

Most people believe action should come
after the outcome is clear.

After the danger is proven.
After the majority agrees.
After the risks are smaller.
After someone else has gone first.

But every turning point in history
was made possible by people
who acted before victory was visible—
not after.

People who wait for certainty never act.

And people who wait for permission
become the ones who later say:

"We didn't know where it was heading."

People imagine history gives warnings,
grace periods,
reminders,
extensions.

It doesn't.

There is no moment labeled:

"Now is the right time to act."

There is only the moment
when action feels too early—
and the moment
when it becomes too late.

The space between those moments
is always smaller than people think.

Most miss it entirely.

Action almost always begins in uncertainty.

That is why so many people delay it.

They assume responsibility will become clearer with time—
when, in fact, time usually narrows
the range of what remains possible.

The Partisans in the forests
did not know if they would survive the week.

The Danes who ferried Jews to Sweden
did not know if they would be shot at sea.

The civil rights marchers
did not know if America would change.

The dissidents in the Soviet bloc
did not know if the wall would fall
in their lifetime.

They acted not because they foresaw victory—
but because living without resistance
was worse than risking failure.

They did not act because they thought they would win.

They acted because they refused
to participate in the lie.

That is the real decision point.

My father did not join the Partisans
because he believed they would defeat the Germans.

He joined because he refused
to let the Germans decide
how he would die—
or how he would live until then.

He chose danger over guaranteed execution.

Most people confuse safety with survival.

He learned the opposite.

Obedience did not mean survival.

Obedience meant a reserved place on the transport.

The only uncertainty was in resistance.

Everything else had already been decided.

Every freedom now treated as normal—
speech, votes, labor rights, civil rights, human rights—

was secured by people who acted
while the outcome was still unknown.

If things get bad enough,
people will be more afraid,
more isolated,
more exhausted,
more controlled,
more dependent.

Resistance does not begin
when the system reaches its worst point.

It begins when people still have something to lose—
and decide they will not lose it quietly.

The people who save a society
are never the ones who waited
until the outcome was certain.

They are the ones who acted
when the future could not yet be predicted—

45

WE ELECT THE LEADERS
WHO REFLECT US

We like to pretend that politicians are the problem.

That they are corrupt,
power-hungry,
self-serving,
dishonest,
immoral—
and that if only we could "vote the bums out,"
everything would change.

But the truth is harder:

We do not elect heroes
in a culture that no longer rewards courage.

We do not elect truth-tellers
in a society that punishes honesty.

Politicians are not the architects of our decline.

They are the mirror.

Every nation gets the leadership
that reflects its present values—
not its highest ideals,
but its actual priorities.

If a society wants decency,
it elects decency.

If a society wants rage,
it elects rage.

If a society wants lies
that feel better than truth,
it elects liars.

Politicians do not invent the culture they exploit.

They study it.

They respond to what gets rewarded,
what gets excused,
and what gets applause.

They tell us what works
because we have already taught them.

We tell ourselves:

"The politicians are the problem. Not us."

But if corrupt leaders keep getting reelected,
it is not because they fooled everyone.

It is because enough people
wanted what they were selling.

We say, "Congress is broken,"

but keep reelecting the broken.

We say, "They don't represent us,"
but they do—
just not the version of us
we wish still existed.

If politicians are dishonest,
it is because honesty stopped winning.

If politicians are cruel,
it is because cruelty gets applause.

If politicians are extremists,
it is because moderation stopped being interesting.

We complain about the poison
while drinking it willingly.

It is easy to say,
"Washington is broken."

It is harder to say:

"It is broken because we broke it—
and kept rewarding what was breaking it."

Democracy does not fail because of one election.

It fails when a society stops demanding character
and starts rewarding performance.

It fails when we choose leaders
who sound like us
instead of leaders
who call us to something better.

If we do not care about democracy,
our leaders won't either.

And they already know it.

They know what we cheer for.

They know what enrages us.

They know which words trigger applause
and which ones are ignored.

They know we will often vote
for the person who makes us feel right
rather than the person who is good.

They know that if the nation wants substance,
it will elect substance.

And if the nation wants performance,
it will elect a performer.

A country does not heal
when it elects better leaders.

It elects better leaders
when it becomes better at what it rewards.

If we want courage,
we must honor it.

If we want truth,
we must reward it.

Leaders do not elevate us.

We elevate them—or we don't.

The government is not separate from the people.

It is the people,
with microphones.

And leadership will not rise
until we do.

4 6

THE CONSTITUTION
CANNOT SAVE US

We talk about the Constitution
as if it is a living guardian—
as if it watches over the nation,
ready to defend our rights,
our freedoms,
our democracy.

But the truth is simpler
and more uncomfortable:

The Constitution is paper.

It cannot defend itself.

It cannot stop corruption, hatred, or tyranny
unless citizens do.

A document cannot save a country.

Only citizens can.

And when citizens stop caring,
the Constitution becomes a relic—
not a protection.

We have convinced ourselves
that the Constitution is self-sustaining—
that it activates automatically
whenever democracy is threatened.

But the Constitution has no voice.

No army.

No power of its own.

It cannot object.

It cannot intervene.

It can only reflect
the beliefs of the people living under it.

If the people honor it,
it has force.

A constitution is never stronger
than the civic culture that sustains it.

Words on a page cannot compel public virtue.

They can only frame it, preserve it,
and reflect whether people still believe
it is worth defending.

Germany had a constitution.

Russia had a constitution.

So do Iran, North Korea, and China.

A constitution does not prevent tyranny.

At most, it delays it—
unless citizens keep it alive.

When people stop defending
the principles inside it,
the words remain—
but the meaning dies.

Rights are not lost
only when governments remove them.

They are lost
when citizens stop believing
they are worth protecting.

No dictator begins
by burning the Constitution.

He begins by persuading people
that the Constitution is in the way.

Once the public accepts
that "extraordinary times" require exceptions,
the paper still exists—
but the republic is already failing.
We say, "The Constitution protects us."

No.

We protect it—or we don't.

The Constitution was never designed
to function on autopilot.

It assumes a moral public.

It assumes people willing
to sacrifice comfort for principle.

If we disappear from that equation,
the system does not save itself.

If we stop protecting the Constitution,
it becomes what it always was:

Paper in a cabinet.
A museum piece.
A historical prop.

The Constitution will not save us.

We will save it—
or we won't.

And if we don't,
history will say what it always says
at the end of a failed republic:

They had the words.
They just stopped believing in them.

THE WORK THAT STILL MATTERS

This chapter is not about what comes next.
It is about the moment
recognition becomes unavoidable.

The day the pattern reached me
was not dramatic.

There were no sirens.
No breaking news.
No single event large enough
to force agreement.

There was only the certainty
that something familiar had returned—
not as history,
but as behavior.

And once you recognize the pattern,
you do not get to unsee it.

That recognition does not grant authority.
It does not guarantee safety.
It simply removes
the excuse of not knowing.

That is where we are now.

Not in the age of destruction.
Not in the age of repair.

We are standing
in the narrowing space between them—
where the future is not yet locked in,
but will be
if enough people remain spectators.

This is the stage
where one truth matters more than any other:

The work that still matters
is the work done
before it is safe,
popular,
or guaranteed to succeed.

We still have voices
they have not yet silenced.

We still have laws
they have not yet rewritten.

We still have elections
they have not yet fully manipulated.

We still have communities
they have not yet completely fractured.

We have fewer tools than before,
but we still have them.

The work now
is to use what still exists
while it still exists.

Because the time will come
when the question shifts from:

What can I do?

to:

What am I legally allowed to do?

And by then,
it will not matter
what anyone wishes
they had done sooner.

What matters in narrowing moments
is not the number of tools remaining,
but whether people still believe
those tools are worth using.

Rights and institutions usually erode
before people realize
how much of their power depended
on exercising them early.

The Work Is Not Theatrical. It Is Relational.

The people who save a democracy
are not the ones
who post the most
or shout the loudest.

They are the ones
who build connections
that propaganda cannot easily break.

The system wants people isolated.
It wants them frightened.
It wants them suspicious of one another.

Because once people are separated,
you do not have to control them.
You only have to keep them apart.

That is why the most subversive act
in a divided society
is simple:

Put in one room
the people who are not supposed to trust each other—
and get them talking anyway.

No government has ever known
how to stop that easily.

Authoritarian systems thrive on fragmentation
because isolation weakens resistance
before resistance can even form.

Relationships do what slogans cannot:

They restore complexity,
break caricature,
and make propaganda harder to sustain.

The Work Is Not About Heroism

One person speaking out feels small.

One person organizing a gathering feels small.
One person refusing to repeat the lie feels small.

But everything that has ever shifted a society
began that way.

The first person to cross the line
is usually isolated.

The third person makes it visible.

And once it becomes visible,
it begins to spread.

Dictators do not fear anger.
They fear people finding each other.

And none of this feels dramatic
when you are inside it.

It feels small.
It feels ordinary.
It feels like nothing will change.

That is why most people wait.

The Biggest Lie of a Collapsing Society

If I do not get involved,
I will be safe.

Silence does not protect you.

It only ensures
that when the consequences arrive,
you will face them
without influence,

without preparation,
and without allies.

There is no path out of history
through non-participation.

There is only the illusion of distance
until distance disappears.

In every collapsing system,
the people who do nothing
are not neutral.

They are the proof
the system needs to continue.

Silence is not agreement.

Silence persists
because it is believed
no one else will speak.

Those who break that illusion
change history.

The work that still matters
is not the work
that guarantees victory.

It is the work
that keeps the door open
long enough
for victory to remain possible.

4 8

THE INFORMATION WAR

There was a time
when journalism was not about winning the argument,
but finding the truth.

When truth was not a product
you could buy, customize,
and stream on demand.

That time is gone.

The media now does not simply report what happens.
It shapes what is believed to have happened.

And the difference between those two things
has become a battleground
on which democracy now fights for its life.

Once, the press understood itself
as the immune system of democracy—
the institution that warned the body

when corruption, deceit, or abuse
entered the bloodstream.

Reporters worked to uncover facts
even when those facts
made their own side uncomfortable.

Today, too often, journalism has traded that purpose for performance.

The headline no longer informs—
it provokes.

The news no longer verifies—
it monetizes.

Outrage has replaced accuracy.
Speed has replaced depth.

Too often, what it is defending
is market share.

The business model changed long before the public fully understood
the consequences.

Once attention became the product, truth stopped being the highest
priority.

We have entered an era
in which journalists have become personalities
and truth has become a stage.

The nightly news is now a contest
of outrage anchors,
moral referees,
and political performers.

They do not sell information.

They sell identity.

When a story breaks,
it no longer needs first
to be understood.

It needs to be framed.

Who benefits?
Who is to blame?

Every event becomes another episode
in the series that keeps viewers loyal.

Each side's media exists, in part,
to reassure its audience
that they are the sane ones,
the patriots,
the morally awake.

And so both sides claim
to defend truth
while helping dismantle
its common meaning.

Truth rarely disappears in one blow.
It is corroded.

A thousand small justifications—commentary, branding, speed,
narrative urgency—
slowly replace the old obligation to verify before inflaming.

Social media promised
to give everyone a voice.

What it gave us instead

was an echo.

The moment truth moved online,
it stopped being sacred
and became content.

And in the digital marketplace,
content does not compete
by being true.

It competes
by being clickable.

Algorithms do not ask
what is accurate.

They ask:

What keeps you here longer?

Outrage does.
Fear does.
Humiliation does.
Hatred does most of all.

So the system learns
what to feed us—
the outrage that tastes like belonging.

Every click refines the recipe.
Every like builds the illusion of consensus.
Every share deepens the division.

The result is a society
where each person lives
inside a customized version of reality—
a personal echo chamber

that feels like truth
because it feels like home.

Democracies require a population capable of recognizing at least some
common reality.

Algorithms profit from keeping citizens emotionally engaged
inside separate ones.

I have watched friends
stop speaking to each other
over headlines.

I have seen families come apart
because they no longer agree
on what is real.

The divide is no longer merely political.
It is existential.

People once argued
about policy and values.

Now they argue
about reality itself.

That is what happens
when media replaces truth
with narrative.

People stop living
in the same world.

It is not just that lies spread faster.
It is that truth becomes lonelier.

The deepest cost of this information war
is not confusion.

It is disconnection.

Propaganda does not simply alter beliefs.
It isolates hearts.

And isolation
is how societies begin
to lose their humanity.

Social media is the first country
in history without borders,
laws,
or shared reality.

It has billions of citizens
but no constitution.

Its armies are hashtags.
Its weapons are words.

In this nation,
truth competes with entertainment
and usually loses.

Because entertainment never asks for courage.
Truth always does.

We once measured civic duty
by what we learned
and what we did with what we learned.

Now it is too often replaced
by performance—

outrage as virtue,
anger as participation,
shaming as justice.

The more emotional your reaction,
the more visible you become.

And the more visible you become,
the more the system rewards you.

We have built a structure
in which reason is disadvantaged
and emotional extremism
is amplified automatically.

In a functioning democracy,
truth is the foundation.

In an attention economy,
truth is friction.

Truth takes time.
It takes patience.
It takes discipline.
It often requires complexity.

Lies scale faster.

And when emotion becomes
the filter for truth,
propaganda becomes almost indistinguishable
from news.

When my parents were alive,
propaganda required control—
of presses, radios, schools.

Today, propaganda requires participation.

We carry it in our pockets.
We feed it with every click.

Once, only journalists
could reliably reach millions.

Now everyone can.

The gatekeepers are gone.
So are the gates.

Freedom of speech
no longer guarantees
the freedom to be heard.

It guarantees the freedom
to be lost in the noise.

We live in a world
where strangers on screens
often feel more credible
than neighbors in person.

Where online following
is confused with authority.

Where every opinion is flattened
into equivalence
and every lie can be amplified instantly.

The internet has made outrage easy
and courage optional.

But moral courage

cannot be tweeted.

It has to be lived.

We mistake visibility for virtue—
as if being seen
is the same thing
as doing something.

It is not.

My parents knew something
we have forgotten:

You cannot defeat lies
with better technology.

You defeat lies
with better people.

My father taught me
that survival was not about cleverness.

It was about character.

The ability to recognize
the difference between truth and convenience
even when truth costs you.

Technology does not create division.
It magnifies what is already there—
fear, resentment, tribalism, pride.

We no longer use media
to understand the world.

This information war
will not be won by censors
or fact-checkers alone.

It will be won—if at all—
by citizens
who still remember
what the word citizen means.

Because no government
can protect truth
if the people prefer lies.

No constitution
can defend reality
if we do not care
what reality is.

Freedom and truth
live or die together.

Once truth becomes a matter of taste,
freedom becomes a matter of time.

That is the danger we face—
not only authoritarianism from above,
but the death of responsibility from below.

We are the first generation
in history to hold
nearly all the world's information
in our hands—
and perhaps the last
that still remembers
how to think before reacting.

If we forget how to distinguish
truth from narrative,
we will not just lose democracy.
We will lose reality.

My parents never imagined a world
where truth could be destroyed
without bullets.

They believed that once humanity saw
what lies could do,
it would never willingly return to them.

But here we are—
repeating their warning
in digital form.

The next generation
will not remember
who spread the lies.

It will remember
who refused to stop them.

And until conscience matters
more than convenience,
truth will remain
what it has always become
in the final hours
of a failing society—
something people used to believe in.

THE ALGORITHM OF DIVISION

What once spread slowly now spreads instantly.

Once, propaganda was crafted by people.

It required intent,
planning,
and the will to deceive.

Dictators needed printers,
filmmakers,
orators,
and control over distribution.

Today, no one needs to invent
the message from scratch.

We built machines
to help us find what we love.

Instead, they learned
what we fear.

They studied every click,
every pause,
every hesitation—
until they could predict
which emotion
would keep us from looking away.

And fear, outrage, and conflict
always win.

The modern algorithm
does not care about truth or falsehood,
right or wrong.

It cares about engagement.

The longer we stay,
the more it learns.

The more it learns,
the longer we stay.

It has no ideology,
no hatred,
no empathy—
but it amplifies
all three.

Every scroll becomes a vote
for what humanity will see next—
and what we will become next.

What used to be propaganda
is now behavioral engineering.

The difference is that we volunteered for it.

We feed the machine our lives
in exchange for convenience,
entertainment,
and belonging.

And it rewards us
with mirrors so perfect
we mistake them for windows.

This is what makes algorithmic division so powerful:

it does not persuade through argument.

It shapes behavior through repetition,
reinforcement,
and emotional reward.

Most do not feel manipulated
because the experience has been personalized
to feel like choice.

In my parents' time,
propaganda required power.

Now, it requires data.

Control has been automated.

No government has to tell us what to think.

We built systems
that learned how to tell us.

The algorithm does not hate Jews,
immigrants,
or any other group in particular.

It simply notices

that anger keeps people online longer.

That fear spreads faster than facts.

That outrage is shared more often than nuance.

That tribal certainty outperforms curiosity.

So it feeds us
what works—
not what is true.

The result is not just misinformation.

It is mass distraction.

The truth is buried
beneath whatever feels
most urgent,
most threatening,
most personal.

Every person now carries
a different world in a pocket.

Two neighbors on the same street
can inhabit entirely different countries
without moving.

One is told
the world is collapsing because of elites.

Another is told
it is collapsing because of the ignorant.

Both feel confirmed
because both feeds
are designed to make each user feel right.

It is commerce.

Division is not a flaw in the system.

It is part of the business model.

Democracy depends on citizens
who can recognize enough common reality
to argue inside the same world.

Algorithms profit
from users who cannot.

There was a time
when people encountered difference by accident.

A newspaper headline.
A voice overheard.
A contradictory conversation.
An unexpected challenge
at a dinner table.

Now chance has been optimized away.

We no longer stumble into disagreement.

We are shielded from it.

Our comfort is curated.

Our outrage is personalized.

Our exposure is managed.

The walls of the digital ghetto
are invisible—
and often stronger
than walls built of stone.

People stay

because leaving would mean
confronting uncertainty again.

And uncertainty
is now experienced as threat.

We traded awareness for affirmation.

We surrendered doubt—
the engine of learning—
for certainty,
which asks nothing of us
but loyalty.

It happened quietly.

The world felt chaotic,
and the algorithm offered order—
an illusion of clarity
made from data and desire.

But order built on outrage
is not stability.

It is sedation.

It keeps people calm enough to consume
and angry enough to return.

My parents lived under tyranny
built by men
who knew exactly what they were doing.

They saw how crowds could be turned
by slogans, rumors, fear.

They understood
how emotion could become
a political weapon.

Today's tyranny
does not wear uniforms
or march in parades.

It lives in code—
invisible,
tireless,
obedient only to what keeps the system running.

If the propaganda of the past
conquered minds through fear,
the propaganda of the present
conquers them through comfort.

The effect is the same:

obedience.

Not always forced obedience.

Chosen obedience.

The kind that feels like freedom
because the menu is personalized.

The algorithm rewards anger.

It punishes empathy.

It teaches people
that listening is weakness,
that compromise is betrayal,
that kindness is unprofitable.

It fragments families,
poisons friendships,
and rewires nervous systems.

And we call it connection.

We confuse visibility with value
and outrage with impact.

When everything becomes performance,
authenticity disappears.

When everyone becomes a brand,
humanity becomes an afterthought.

For those of us born from survivors,
manipulation feels familiar.

We know what it means
when reality is rewritten.

When whole populations
turn away from suffering
because it is easier not to see.

The algorithm does not threaten
with guns or camps.

But it dulls the moral reflex
that once made people stand up to both.

It numbs us into believing
that awareness is action,
that sharing is resistance,
that posting outrage
is the same as changing the world.

And like every illusion of safety,
it disappears
the moment truth demands courage.

We may not be able to dismantle the algorithm.

But we can starve it.

Every time we pause before reacting,
every time we check the source,
every time we refuse to share
what only fuels anger—
we weaken the machine.

Its power depends on our attention.

It has no strength
without our eyes,
our clicks,
our time.

The only thing it cannot replace
is conscience.

Because conscience cannot be coded.

My parents' generation understood
what happens
when lies become normal
and silence becomes survival.

They saw how easily truth vanishes
when emotion becomes
the only language people trust.

They knew
that the loss of truth

always begins
with the loss of empathy.

Our battlefield is different.

The moral test is not.

They had to fight propaganda
with courage.

We must fight algorithms
with awareness,
discipline,
and refusal.

In the end,
machines do not destroy humanity.

Humans do—
when they let machines
define what being human means.

The Holocaust began
with words people chose to believe.

Today, belief spreads faster than ever,
unburdened by evidence
and accelerated by code.

History no longer merely repeats itself.

It uploads itself.

We cannot return
to a pre-digital world.

But we can remember

what the digital world forgot:

Truth is relational,
not algorithmic.

Every generation is tested
by what comforts it most.

Ours is being tested
by the comfort of illusion.

And the only way through
is to feel again—
to care,
to think,
to question.

Because freedom does not disappear
only when it is taken away.

It disappears
when people stop noticing
that it is gone.

5 0

CULTURE WARS

By now you see how this connects.

By the time people give a phenomenon a name,
it has usually been unfolding
for a long time.

That is true
of what we now call the culture wars.

Culture wars are not merely arguments
about taste, language, or politics.

They are conflicts over belonging.

Over who is allowed to exist
without explanation.

Who is trusted by default.

At their core,

culture wars are battles over hierarchy under pressure.

They erupt when systems
that once controlled access
to legitimacy, opportunity, or moral standing
feel that control slipping.

One of the most persistent myths
is that politicians created our culture wars.

They did not.

Politicians follow permission.

They rarely invent it.

Long before laws change,
norms change.

Long before leaders act,
communities signal
what they will tolerate,
excuse,
or quietly enforce—
in schools,
boards,
religious institutions,
nonprofits,
neighborhoods,
professional organizations.

They model behavior.

What later appears on the national stage is frequently a larger, louder
version of what communities have already normalized in smaller spaces
where fewer people are paying attention.

I did not need theory

to recognize this pattern.

I recognized it
when I saw it again—
not in a corporation this time,
but in Jewish communal life.

That recognition was deeply unsettling.

As a Jew,
I expected shared memory
to act as a safeguard.
I expected history
to function as a brake.

I expected that a people
shaped by exclusion, silence, and persecution
would be especially alert
to the early signs
of those same behaviors.

Instead, I encountered something familiar.

Boards protecting power
rather than principle.

People quietly pushed out
for refusing to conform.
Different moral vocabulary.

Same pattern.

I watched rabbis define who belonged
and who did not—
not through theology,
but through conformity.

I watched lay leaders—
people entrusted
with ethical and fiduciary responsibility—
look away
when principle was violated.

In other settings,
such failures would have meant
loss of trust or removal from leadership.

Instead, silence was rewarded
and compliance preserved.

What troubled me most
was not disagreement.

It was certainty.

The assumption
that those in power were right
because they were in power.

The expectation
that belonging required alignment.

The belief
that moral intent excused conduct.

I saw it again
in other nonprofits as well—
leaders convinced of their righteousness,
demanding loyalty rather than engagement,
treating questions as threats
instead of obligations.

And I watched many of these same people

condemn authoritarian behavior in Washington
while practicing smaller, quieter versions
of the same thing.

Different scale.
Different terms.

It plays out the same.

That is how patterns survive.

Not because people believe themselves evil—
but because they believe themselves exempt.

Both the left and the right
now operate with rules—spoken and unspoken—
about who belongs.

Each side defines acceptable language.
Acceptable doubts.
Acceptable histories.
Acceptable loyalties.

Each side increasingly treats
fellow Americans
not as people to persuade,
but as people to disqualify.

The symbols differ.
The moral stories differ.

But once disagreement becomes disqualification,
the culture has already shifted.

A society that polices belonging
is no longer debating ideas.

It is enforcing identity.

And enforcement always escalates.

More than a decade ago,
I moved to a rural community.

Politically, we do not agree on everything.

Ideologically, we are all over the map.

And yet, as a Jew,
I feel safer and more welcome here
than I did in the city where I once lived.

Here, I am treated as a human being first—
not a label,
not a test case,
not a symbol.

People attend the sessions I conduct
on the history of hatred toward Jews,
the Holocaust,
the Israel-Palestinian conflict,
and the health of a democracy—
not to posture,
but to understand.

In the city,
very few showed interest.

Here, people show up.

In smaller communities, relationships can still interrupt
abstraction.
People still know one another through daily life rather than through
labels alone.

That does not eliminate division, but it makes dehumanization harder
to sustain because categories have to compete with familiarity.

There are two kinds of silence.

There is quiet action—
the kind that saved lives during the Holocaust.

Farmers who hid families.
Neighbors who did not turn people in.
Clerks who forged papers.
Strangers who gave warnings, food, clothing, or a single weapon.

And then there is the silence of inaction.

The silence that hides behind slogans.
The silence that substitutes words for risk.

No one saved my parents
by saying, "Never forget."

Those words, without action,
change nothing.

Memory without action
does not interrupt patterns.

It preserves them.

This book is not asking people
to pick a side.

It is asking them
to recognize a pattern.

The same behaviors

that hollowed out institutions
now hollow out communities.

The same instincts
that punished truth-tellers
inside organizations
now punish dissenters in public life.

The question is not
whether culture wars will end.

They always do.

The question is
how much damage we accept
before they do—
and whether we are willing
to recognize ourselves in the mirror
before blaming someone else.

51

LIVING BETWEEN TWO WORLDS

Culture does not announce itself.

It teaches you
through what is normal,
what is invisible,
and what you are expected
not to question.

I learned this long before anyone used the term culture wars.

I learned it by living inside one of the largest, most powerful
corporations in the world at the height of its success—
and, at the same time,
living in a second world
that most of the people around me
never noticed or inhabited.

I started working at Kodak in 1980.

That year alone, Kodak hired roughly 2,000 engineers in Rochester.

The company was booming.

Buildings were going up everywhere.

Entire production lines were being designed, built, installed, expanded.

In Rochester, 66,000 people worked for Kodak.

45,000 were at my plant alone.

Kodak was not a company.

It was a city.

It had its own power plant, water system, fire department, bus system, rail lines, and internal services.

It even ran one of the largest industrial food service operations in the world.

Wherever you worked, there was a cafeteria nearby.

Engineers, technicians, trades, hourly workers, administrators—

everyone ate there.

Everyone—
except senior management.

There was a management dining room.

It mattered.

Not because the food was better—though it was.

The menu changed daily.

You could order almost anything.

Executive chefs prepared meals on request.

But the food wasn't the point.

The point
was who belonged there.

The first time I saw it was through work.

I was assigned to projects involving senior managers, and they would suggest meeting there.

Guests could be invited—

as long as they fit the profile.

Only white men.

No women.

The waitstaff were not professional servers.

They were executive secretaries.

These were often the best secretaries—
women who had advanced as far as the system allowed
below senior management.

Serving in the dining room
was not a promotion.

It was part of being considered
for executive secretary positions.

It was an audition.

How attractive you were.

How you served male executives.

How you dressed.

How well you tolerated comments, flirting, and jokes.

These women carried departments behind the scenes—
tracking, fixing, coordinating everything.

That was the culture.

What defines a culture is rarely written policy.

It is the set of behaviors that become normal
because they are repeated without consequence.

The first week I was at Kodak,
the Jewish holidays were coming up.

I asked my supervisor what the policy was for time off.

He looked at me blankly.

He had never heard of the holidays.

That moment came before anything else—
before projects, relationships, or hierarchy.

And, in that instant, I understood what had happened.

I had revealed something
that did not fit the assumed norm.

Before he could respond, I backed away.

"I'll just use vacation days."

Conversation over.

Not long after, a Jewish colleague pulled me aside.

Quietly and urgently.

"Don't tell people you're Jewish."

"If the wrong people find out, it will destroy your career."

That sentence shaped the next twenty years.

I learned how to pass.

How to live in two worlds at once.

To the outside, I looked like a white Christian man.

I was treated like one.

I received the assumptions that came with it—competence, belonging,
safety.

But I knew it was conditional.

And because I could move between those worlds,
I saw what others did not.

I watched how Black employees were treated—

especially in skilled trades.

Training denied.

Advancement blocked.

They were kept as helpers.

Racist slurs were written openly.

Management saw them.

Nothing happened.

I watched Hispanic and Asian employees.

They were present,
but rarely mentored,
rarely advanced,
rarely seen as leadership material.

I watched women—
on job sites and in offices.

Sexual jokes were routine.

Harassment was normalized.

Competence was questioned
even when they were doing the work.

This was not a few bad actors.

It was structural.

It was normalized.

And all the while, the company believed itself fair.

Systems rarely sustain inequality by accident.

They sustain it through habits, expectations, and decisions
that feel routine to those who benefit from them.

I did not start as a mentor.

I became a manager first.

Only then did I begin mentoring—intentionally—
because I finally had the authority to act.

One moment made it clear.

My secretary had just given birth.

She asked for additional unpaid leave.

I asked my manager.

He was furious.

"No."

"She has to use vacation."

When I called her back, she wasn't surprised.

"I knew what the answer would be."

That was the moment.

If I wanted to lead fairly,
I could not keep asking permission
from people who did not believe fairness mattered.

So I stopped asking.

I approved leave.

I approved training.

I assigned real work
to people the system had written off.

They succeeded.

Not because standards changed.

Because opportunity had been withheld.

Most people say Kodak failed
because it missed digital.

That is wrong.

Kodak failed because of its culture.

People inside knew.

You could hear it in cafeterias, hallways, and private conversations.

We were not blind.

Ten years before I left,
I told a manager Kodak would go bankrupt.

He told me I was crazy.

"We're the world leader."

As if leadership guaranteed survival.

For decades, layoffs hit workers.

Hourly.
Technical.
Engineering.

Gone.

Management—protected.

Organizations shrank to a fraction.

Leaders stayed.

Pay stayed.

Benefits stayed.

Workers lost everything.

Leadership lost almost nothing.

They believed workers were the problem.

That belief killed Kodak.

Today, fewer than 1,000 people remain in Rochester.

From 66,000 to 1,000.

Organizations rarely break down because the problem is not seen.

They break down because the people with power refuse to accept
what others already understand.

Because I lived in both worlds—
inside the dominant culture
and outside it—
I saw the pattern early.

Kodak was not just a company.

It was a rehearsal.

And it taught me what happens
when power protects itself,
truth is ignored,
and stability is mistaken for justice.

52

THE FUTURE STILL
WORTH BUILDING

The story of every democracy
is the story of people deciding—again and again—
that freedom is worth the work.

It is never finished.

America was never a completed project.

It was an experiment.

Not perfect.

But always reaching.

From the beginning,
the language made that clear—
a more perfect union,
not a finished one.

Somewhere along the way,
we mistook comfort for progress.

We assumed ideals could maintain themselves.

That the Constitution would defend itself.

That the next generation
would automatically inherit courage.

But experiments only survive
when participants keep showing up.

The moment we stop tending the promise,
the promise fades.

The future still worth building
will not come from slogans.

It will come from the same materials
that built everything before:

Honesty.
Empathy.
Courage.

We must return to something simple—
decency practiced,
not proclaimed.

Progress Is Not Permanent

For most of my life,
I believed progress was permanent.

That once earned,
it could not be undone.

That was wrong.

Progress is not a possession.

It is a practice.

It requires maintenance.

And sometimes
confrontation with ourselves.

Every generation inherits something unfinished.

The question is never whether the work exists—
it is whether the generation
accepts responsibility for it.

Rebuilding does not begin in Washington.

It begins in:

Kitchens.
Classrooms.
Town halls.
Communities.

It begins
when people speak across fear.

When they listen to understand
instead of to win.

No nation heals from the top down.

It heals
when citizens remember
what "We the people" actually means.

I still see it.

In libraries
where people sit through uncomfortable conversations.

In teachers
who insist truth is not partisan.

In communities
that serve anyone who shows up.

That is the future still worth building—
held together
by people
who have not given up on decency.

My parents did not finish the work.

They cleared the path.

They created a world
where people could argue safely,
believe freely,
build without terror.

They handed us possibility.

Now we decide
whether we deserve to keep it.

The moral arc does not bend by itself.

It bends
when people act.

When teachers teach honestly.

When journalists tell truth.

When voters demand character.

The world they rebuilt was not flawless.

But it was built on belief—
that humanity could be trusted again.

That belief is our inheritance.

What we do with it
will be our legacy.

The future is being shaped—now—
by people
who refuse to give up on decency.

Freedom is not a gift.

It is a discipline.

And rebuilding begins
with the living.

53

THE RESPONSIBILITY
OF THE LIVING

The future is never guaranteed.

It is rented by the living—
paid for in attention,
courage,
and truth.

Every generation receives the same inheritance:

A world built by others,
and fragile enough
to be undone.

I did not ask
to carry this history.

But history does not wait for volunteers.

It assigns responsibility
through survival.

When my parents gave me their silence,
I thought it was peace.

It was not.

It was unfinished pain.

Writing *Miracles Through Hell*
was my way of translating that silence.

This book continues that work—
turning inheritance
into instruction.

Every failure begins
when people decide
truth can wait.

"I'm tired of hearing about it."

"That was long ago."

"It's not my problem."

That is how forgetting begins.

Our responsibility
is to interrupt that.

Not perfectly.

But persistently.

My parents survived
because people acted.

Not heroically in the way stories tell it.
But repeatedly.

Small acts.

Food.
Clothing.
Information.
Weapons.

Those small acts made larger ones possible.

Resistance is built
on accumulation.

There is good silence—
silence paired with action.

And bad silence—
silence paired with avoidance.

Bad silence
is how patterns lock in.

"Never Again" has become a ritual.

But words do nothing
without action.

Memory alone
does not interrupt history.

It preserves it.

If the phrase means anything,
it means responsibility.

Condemnation rarely changes ignorance.

Dialogue does.

Relationships do.

I have seen it.

In conversations with non-Jewish audiences.

Again and again, the same response:

"I had no idea."

That moment matters.

It is where change begins.

Today, people believe they are engaged
because they repost outrage.

That is not action.

It costs nothing.

Risks nothing.

Changes nothing.

History is not changed by agreement.

It is changed by interruption.

Small acts still matter.

They always have.

They always will.

And something we have forgotten:

Talking to each other.

Small acts interrupt big patterns.

Echoes of History focuses on understanding the patterns that shift
norms, behaviors, and societies over time.

It explains how people slowly adapt to emotional environments around them—
often without realizing they are changing too.

How fear spreads.
How outrage spreads.
How people slowly stop seeing one another as human beings.

But understanding the pattern is not enough.

When people remain silent,
emotionally withdraw,
or stop believing they can influence anything,
the current pattern remains the future.

That is how societies drift.

Not because most people consciously choose where the pattern leads—
but because they slowly adapt to it
until it no longer feels unusual at all.

Patterns reveal where societies are heading
long before the consequences fully appear.

And if left alone long enough,
they become culture.

That is why the most important question is not simply:
"What is happening to America?"

The deeper question is:
"What kind of society are we becoming?"

Is this where we want the pattern to lead?

Is this the kind of emotional atmosphere we want to live inside
every day?

Is this the kind of country we want to leave our children and grandchildren?

Because societies are shaped not only by governments,
institutions,
or the forces competing for our attention.

They are also shaped by ordinary human behavior repeated every day.

How people treat each other.

How people respond to fear.

How quickly anger replaces understanding.

How people disagree.

What people normalize.

What people excuse.

What people remain silent about.

Healthy societies are not held together by perfection.

They are held together by patterns that reinforce trust,
empathy,
restraint,
truth,
shared responsibility,
and the belief that fellow citizens still belong to the same human community.

And unhealthy societies drift when those patterns are replaced by fear,
humiliation,
emotional conflict,
manipulation,
and the belief that other people are no longer fully human unless they agree with us.

Small repeated behaviors become culture over time.

That is how unhealthy patterns spread.

But it is also how healthier patterns spread.

Empathy spreads.

Calm spreads.

Humanity spreads.

The future is not shaped only by leaders.

It is shaped by whether ordinary people remain conscious enough to recognize unhealthy patterns before they fully become the culture.

But once people become conscious of the pattern,
they begin choosing again.

The living cannot change the past.

But we decide what comes next.

My parents survived the fire.

I am living in the smoke.

But I still see light—
in the small acts
people continue to choose.

That is the responsibility of the living.

To carry it forward.

And now,
it belongs to us.

EPILOGUE: THE SMALL ACTS THAT SAVED THE WORLD

History remembers the wars, the marches, the treaties.

But what truly saves civilization
are the moments when one person refuses to look away.

A loaf of bread slipped through a fence.

A family that hides another family.

A teacher who refuses to change a lesson
because truth matters more than comfort.

A neighbor who says, "Not in my town."

These small, ordinary choices
have always held the world together
when everything else was falling apart.

We think history is written by power.

It isn't.

It's written by conscience—
and conscience begins
with one decision at a time.

I think often about my father's sled—
how something so simple
became a vessel for survival.

It was a token of faith
that courage could still matter
in a world built to destroy it.

That same faith appears in every generation,
in forms that look nothing like heroism.

Today, it might be a journalist printing one more story,
a student walking out rather than cheering for cruelty,
a citizen protecting the truth
when silence would be safer.

None of them will have their names
or likenesses carved in stone.

But civilization stands
because they existed.

After writing *Miracles Through Hell*
and then this book,
I see the pattern clearer than ever:

The past erodes from indifference,
and it heals through connection.

That is why I cannot stop writing—
because remembering is not enough
if it doesn't reach the living.

I want this work to grow beyond me—
to include the voices of others:

survivors,
second-generation witnesses,
educators,
and those who have seen new forms of hate rise
and refused to let it pass.

There are teachers
who teach the Holocaust as living moral history.

There are young people
refusing to inherit their parents' silence.

They are all part of this same thread.

We need to gather these stories
as reminders
that the future is never hopeless
as long as people act.

A book can become a conversation.

A conversation can become a movement.

And a movement can become a moral shift.

Most people never see themselves as brave.

But courage rarely announces itself as bravery.

It appears as hesitation
followed by a choice.

It is the teacher
who keeps her job by telling the truth anyway.

The parent
who raises a child to ask questions.

The faith leader
who refuses to preach hate
even when it fills seats.

The neighbor
who says hello
to someone everyone else avoids.

The writer
who keeps writing
when others have given up on listening.

These are the acts
that save the world.

Not all at once.

Not loudly.

But persistently—
the way daylight insists on returning
even after the longest night.

If this book ends anywhere,
let it end here—
in gratitude.

To those who carried light through horror.

To those who refused to forget
when forgetting was easier.

History will not remember every name.

But the future will remember
that they existed.

Because every act of decency,
every refusal to hate,
every word spoken in defense of truth
is not small.

It is civilization in practice.

We will never know
all the lives saved
by small acts of courage.

But we do know this:

Without them,
the world would already be gone.

And so the story continues,
and the spark refuses to die.

As long as one person
still believes courage matters,
the world is not beyond saving.

AUTHOR'S NOTE

I did not plan to write this book.

After I finished *Miracles Through Hell*,
I thought I had finally done what I was meant to do:

tell my parents' story,
honor their survival,
and give voice to the silence
inside which I grew up.

I believed that was the book I owed them—
and that once it was written,
the weight I had carried all my life
would finally lift.

But something unexpected happened.

In telling their story,
I began to see the world they survived returning
in new shapes,

new languages,
and new excuses.

And suddenly, the past was no longer finished.

It was knocking on the present—
and too many people were not hearing it.

So this book is not a sequel.

It is the result of what happens
when the child of survivors recognizes
that memory alone is not enough.

Because there comes a moment
when remembering becomes a form of looking away.

And there comes a moment
when the responsibility of the living
is not to mourn the past,
but to interrupt its return.

My parents did not survive
so I could write one book
about what happened to them.

They survived
so I would recognize
when it was happening again.

And it is.

Not in the same uniforms.

Not in the same speeches.

But in the same patterns.

The same silence.

The same denial.

The same belief
that "it can't happen here."

The same comfort
that keeps people from acting
until it no longer matters.

My father didn't survive
because he believed
the world would fix itself.

He survived because he understood
that when danger becomes real,
you either act—
or you become part of its proof.

I am alive
because he didn't wait.

And I wrote this book
because I will not either.

This is not a book of answers.

It is a book of warnings—
and a handoff.

My parents' generation is gone.

Their survivors are almost gone.

The world that remembers them is disappearing.

But the danger that created their suffering

is not disappearing.

It is only evolving.

I am a second-generation survivor.

That means I inherited not only their trauma,
but their instructions:

Do not let the world pretend it didn't happen.

Do not let the world say it didn't know.

Do not let silence become normal.

This book is my way
of keeping that promise.

Whatever comes next—
for this country,
for the world—
will not be decided by the dead.

It will be decided by us.

And if there is one thing I have learned
from a lifetime of carrying inherited fire,
it is this:

The past does not repeat
because we remember too little.

It repeats
because we act too late.

My parents did not get the world they deserved.

But as long as I am alive,

I will fight for the future
their suffering demanded.

I owe them that.

I owe the next generation more.

—Jerry Elman

SOURCES AND
SUGGESTED READING

This book was not written as a history lesson, but as a warning built on history.

For readers who want to go deeper—into the Holocaust itself, into the psychology of collapsing democracies, and into the ways ordinary people become participants in systems they never imagined—the works below offer clarity, witness, and truth without denial or simplification.

They do not all agree.

But they all illuminate the same patterns.

To understand the Holocaust through those who lived it

Night — **Elie Wiesel**
A survivor's testimony stripped to its moral core—a book that refuses to let the dead be reduced to statistics.

Man's Search for Meaning — **Viktor Frankl**
A psychiatrist and survivor explains not only what happened in the camps, but how human beings stay alive in the absence of hope.

***The Drowned and the Saved* — Primo Levi**
A piercing reflection on memory, complicity, and what it means when the unthinkable becomes normal.

***Survival in Auschwitz* — Primo Levi**
Not just a record of suffering, but of what dehumanization does to the human self.

To understand how societies slide into authoritarianism

***They Thought They Were Free* — Milton Mayer**
Interviews with ordinary Germans reveal how people slowly learned to live comfortably inside a dictatorship—one small adjustment at a time.

***Ordinary Men* — Christopher Browning**
A study of how regular, non-fanatic men became mass murderers—not through ideology, but through conformity and obedience.

***The Origins of Totalitarianism* — Hannah Arendt**
A foundational analysis of how propaganda, isolation, and manufactured division make freedom feel unnecessary.

To understand the warning signs in our own time

***On Tyranny* — Timothy Snyder**
Twenty short lessons drawn from 20th-century history—a manual for recognizing when democracy is being replaced by spectacle and fear.

***How Democracies Die* — Steven Levitsky and Daniel Ziblatt**
A modern study of countries that did not collapse from revolution, but from citizens turning against each other.

***The Road to Unfreedom* — Timothy Snyder**
A look at how truth is eroded, lies replace reality, and nations become captive to narratives instead of facts.

This list is not exhaustive.

It is an invitation.

To see more clearly.
To question more deeply.
To recognize the patterns before they harden into consequences.

ABOUT THE AUTHOR

Jerry Elman is an author, educator, and second-generation Holocaust survivor whose work focuses on the intersection of memory, trauma, and the repeating patterns of history. He is the author of *Miracles Through Hell*, the true account of his parents' survival during the Holocaust and the silence that shaped his childhood. That book opened the door to conversations with thousands of readers—Jews and non-Jews—who recognized themselves in the inherited wounds of history.

This book continues that work, not by retelling the past, but by confronting the way it is returning in new forms. Elman writes for those who were never taught the full story, for those who were taught to forget it, and for those who refuse to accept that "Never Again" was meant to be a slogan instead of an active responsibility.

His writing is driven by a single unbroken thread: the belief that the children of survivors carry not only their parents' trauma, but their unfinished warning—and that silence is no longer an option.

He speaks and writes to audiences who may never have met a survivor, but who now live in the world their survival was meant to protect.

AUTHOR BIO

Jerry Elman is an author, educator, and second-generation Holocaust survivor whose work examines how historical patterns repeat across societies, institutions, and individual lives. He is the author of *Miracles*

Through Hell, which documents his parents' survival of the Holocaust and the lasting impact of inherited trauma across generations.

Elman has spent years speaking to community groups, libraries, and schools about the Holocaust, moral responsibility, and the early warning signs of societal breakdown. A former engineer, business owner, and nonprofit leader, he brings a systems-level perspective to questions of culture, power, and accountability. His writing bridges history, psychology, and lived experience, focusing on how silence, fear, and conformity shape both private identity and public life. He lives in Canadice, New York.